SILVER FOX

SILVER FOX

A Dating Guide for Women over 50

Elaine Ruth Mitchell

iUniverse, Inc.
New York   Bloomington

Silver Fox
A Dating Guide for Women over 50

iUniverse books may be ordered through booksellers or by contacting:

iUniverse
1663 Liberty Drive
Bloomington, IN 47403
www.iuniverse.com
1-800-Authors (1-800-288-4677)

Because of the dynamic nature of the Internet, any Web addresses or links contained in this book may have changed since publication and may no longer be valid.

ISBN: 978-1-4502-0870-3 (sc)
ISBN: 978-1-4502-0872-7 (dj)
ISBN: 978-1-4502-0871-0 (ebk)

Printed in the United States of America

iUniverse rev. date: 6/18/2010

Contents

Acknowledgements

Friends and family have supported me mightily. All the women in my journaling groups have given me laughter, tears, wonderful writing, fascinating stories, and feedback. My friend, Lola Rasminsky, has been the angel of my career as a teacher of journaling.

My writing partner, Kim Aubry, gave me valuable editing help, as did the dear friends who read the book through its multiple drafts: Susan Chapman, Laura Hickey, Liz Martin, and Lyndsay Moffitt. Much appreciation for suggestions from Arei Bierstock, Monika Ghent, Sheila LeGacy, and my sister Barbara Mitchell Pollock. My sweetheart, David Oved, and my daughter, Rachel Matlow, gave me great ideas and editing, and my son, Josh Matlow, proffered expert marketing advice and help. To the gals at Magpie, Cathy and Angela, for the foxy silver motorcycle jacket. Thanks to my ex-husband, Ted Matlow, for proofing, forbearance and friendship.

This book is dedicated to the memory of my mother and father, in gratitude, love and respect.

Preface

○ ○

You need to claim the events of your life to make yourself yours. When you truly possess all you have been and done, which may take some time, you are fierce with reality.

Florida Scott-Maxwell   (1884-1979)
Writer, suffragist, psychologist, actor.

I want to share my transformation from "ugly duckling" into Silver Fox. It took me from puberty to post-menopause to come into my own as a confident woman. Now, in my sixties, I find I am sought after.

Most books about later-life dating are cautionary. All those tales of nasty demographics, of how there are so few men out there for so many wonderful women, of loneliness and regrets, of settling for companionship, and not always the finest. But I have also heard and read stories of unexpected happiness, of finding the best love, the love of a lifetime, after age fifty, or sixty, or even seventy. My mother found true love with a younger man when she was eighty-eight.

It is important to remember that demographics can be read in many ways. If you have, say, a good twenty years ahead of you and are not impatient, which is more likely—a) that you couldn't find someone to love, or b) that you could? Even if there are more women than men "in the dating trenches", not all of us want to give up our freedom for a man, or have let go of desperation or anger, or have much trust in men. Not all of us are ready to receive love—yet.

You can benefit from just reading *Silver Fox,* even though I believe that journaling is easy and life-altering. You don't have to be a "good writer". You don't have to write a whole lot. You just have to move your pen towards the life you want.

You can write yourself into a Silver Fox.

I bring to this book my expertise as a teacher of journaling and as a journal keeper. I have led consciousness-raising writing workshops for twenty-two years and have kept a journal since I was nine years old.

Silver Fox arose out of a healthy sense of outrage that women of a superior age are undervalued. Discouraged by the ageism in our society, many women have blocked themselves from going after what they want. For all of you who desire sexual love and are thinking of giving up, I hope that this book can help you get in touch with your true needs and resist the negative messages we aging women constantly receive.

Even the term "Silver Fox" is more often associated with men than women. Older men are still considered sexy, and are supported in their natural desire to find sexual partners. Older women are given different messages. Only a young woman is a "fox".

Who, or what, is a female Silver Fox, you may ask?

A Silver Fox has lived long enough to have ripened into her sleek and silver self. She is ready to live and love fiercely and fearlessly. She is in the prime of her life because she knows who she is. Knows what she has to give, and knows how to give it.

A Silver Fox has never felt better about men because she is finally strong enough not to be falsely compliant. She can appreciate men from a peer position. She is a grown up and she can attract other grown ups.

Silver Foxes come in various forms and have eclectic tastes. One fox might put on a sexy push-up bra under her T-shirt, another, a sports bra under a vintage cashmere sweater. She might strut in stilettos or stride in sneakers with orthodics. A Silver Fox is forever alluring without working to look young. She knows she is a sexual being until it's over (and it's not over until it's over!). She is attractive because she has style, charm, confidence, élan, a capacity for love, a warm smile, and a straight honest manner. Her energy and aura are magnetic.

A Silver Fox treats herself well. She wears only what looks and feels great. She uses her best dishes and silverware—no more keeping stuff "for good". She buys affordable luxuries: hand-milled soaps, huge bunches of dried lavender, Prosecco and pinot noir, fresh flowers, and Belgian chocolate. She doesn't have to be rich to be good at artful living.

The Silver Fox has hit the silver screen. Catherine Deneuve, Susan Sarandon, Diane Keaton are magnificently aging stars. Our world is full of women of a certain age who are attractive, productive and having the time of their lives.

I will guide you on an expedition that I have been on for much of my life—the search for self through journaling. The more we become our true selves, the more we become irresistible. Putting down real thoughts and feelings, reading those thoughts and feelings, listening to our words, honouring the unvarnished truth—journaling in this way leads to love and compassion for self and other. Our words lay down a trail to success, in love and in life.

Don't hold yourself back from this journey. It's about living life to the fullest, expanding into new situations, new friendships, and perhaps love. There are risks: discomfort, looking foolish, dejection, heartbreak. But the rewards are also there for you, whatever your age.

I have chosen to limit this book to my experiences as a heterosexual middle-class North American woman. While I have many friends who have had other experiences, it would not be honest to claim those as my own. I have tried to be conscious of my privilege and biases, but acknowledge that they will be present.

If you are holding this book in your hands, you are ready to transform into a Silver Fox. I am pleased to be with you as you start a new chapter of your life.

Life is either a daring adventure or nothing.

Helen Keller

-1-
Still dating
(after all these years)

○ ○

Men are my kind of people. Mae West

I have been dating for an astonishing—to me—nineteen years since my divorce.

When I left my marriage, I did it without a therapist and without a lover. I left when I could have stayed, and been "safe" and comfortable both emotionally (in a certain cramped way) and financially. But the marriage wasn't good, and I wanted a different life. I wanted to be my best self. I was forty-six, thinking that I might be alone forever, but that would be better than twisting myself into a lesser person than I could be.

The messages I got from the media told me I would probably remain on my own for the rest of my life. Well-meaning self-help books kindly warned that the chances of finding true love were slim. Friends who were divorced were not encouraging, and an analyst pal told me categorically that I would have a lot of trouble finding dates at my age. I believed all these harbingers of my fate, but decided to take my chances. I was brave, I think. And I found it exciting to go out into the world with little money, and only myself to bet on.

My experience has been the opposite of the over-the-hill, overlooked mythology. Although I am not magazine beautiful,

1

I have simply not had a problem meeting men and attracting men. In fact, I have actually attracted more men more frequently as I age. Many of my friends and acquaintances have had the same experience.

Self-esteem came late and slow into my life. I was confident until puberty and then I lost myself. In high school I was a nerd who edited the yearbook and watched only depressing foreign films, protecting my weak inner self with intellectual pretensions. I didn't know how to flirt. I wore a peace button and a tweed skirt made by my tailor father instead of the "in" felt skirt with poodle and rhinestone eyes. I believed I should be a virgin when I married (*your ace in the hole*, my mother instructed when I was thirteen). I danced with unlimited inhibition, yearned for unattainable crushes, read Sartre in French in cafés, hoping to attract cute guys, and marched in unflattering clothes at demos with that same goal. I was terrified that a boy would like me for my body rather than my mind.

I was still insecure in my twenties and thirties, forty before I truly believed I was attractive, in my late forties before I had sexual confidence, fifty-eight before I splurged on lacey Parisian lingerie, and sixty-three before I began my first really sane relationship with a man.

I have discovered that finding love is deeply connected to understanding how much we older women have to offer. We tend to be more spontaneous, sure of ourselves, successful, generous, fun, and evolved than our younger selves. We take things less personally. We have the perspective to take life by the horns.

It also helps to realize that older men often make better partners than younger men. Perhaps because they have experienced pain and loss, many older single men crave connection and intimacy and are willing to engage in the give and take of an equal relationship rather than expecting a woman to fit into their lives. This can be a breath of fresh air for those of us who have left unhappy unions and fear that relationships with men are doomed or that men never change.

I've met many women who would like a man in their lives but have given up. They don't want a man to see them naked (as if a man who really likes a woman and finds her naked in his bed is going to be critical). They feel it's beneath them to go online or place an ad for what they want. They're too embarrassed to go to singles events. They second guess themselves out of the game before they play (too old, too fat, too needy, men are bastards, men want younger women). All these things may have a grain of truth until a good guy (one definition—a man who wants more than arm candy and phallic reassurance) meets a woman who interests him or excites him. He may have biases, but he wants to experience chemistry with someone as much as you do.

At mid-life and after, most of us who are single have considerable baggage, and the knowledge of the sharp U-turns happy roads sometimes take. The adventure of falling in love, of going into wild territory with only desire and courage, is scary for many of us. We need some version of Ariadne's thread, the stringing of words into meanings, to guide us there, and perhaps back to ourselves.

In Greek legend, Ariadne gave Theseus a magic ball of thread that led him out of a labyrinth to safety. "Ariadne's thread" is now often used to mean the keeping of a record to help solve a problem, let's say whether or not to become involved with a new man. Our record—a *Still Dating Diary*—generates and identifies options in approaching the problem. It allows us to try many ways of proceeding, including backtracking. A written record of our thoughts, feelings, and actions, there for review and reflection, can guide us out of the mazes we get lost in.

A search for sexual love fares better with reflection. We can use the journal as a teaching mirror, a way of tuning in to what we're really doing, feeling, thinking, desiring. Journaling allows us to accept and process our feelings. We don't have to continually express them in the same old conversations with friends, or repress them until they fester or explode. We can keep writing until we centre ourselves.

I teach journaling. My work is to empower people through their own words. In the years when I was unconsciously preparing to leave my marriage, I taught courses entitled "Finding Your True Voice". I felt passionate about that theme. Who better to teach the finding of that ground note—the true voice—than I, an older sister, a psychological parent to my needy parents, a giver of advice, a teacher who worked to inspire beginning writers. Later, I realized why I had so much energy for those courses and workshops, and why I really meant it when I would say, "I'm learning as much from you as you are from me" to my adult and teenage students. Some of them revealed truths about their lives that I was able to connect to my own life, and I admired their courage in naming what I would have been afraid to say.

I have always been verbal, and think of myself as an open and straightforward person. Yet, on rereading my own writing, both in my fiction and my journals, I saw how difficult it had been for me to say my truth when it came to the hard things (like telling a man what I wanted or didn't want in bed). Over the years I realized I needed to open the invisible door to my "real" voice.

Journaling has been one of the ways I have connected with this voice. By journaling, I was in effect talking with myself. I asked and answered many questions. I looked into the dark corners of my life, the insecurity and masked depression, the anger and self-righteous judgment. I realized that I had avoided seeing those corners because they subverted the personality I wanted to present to the world (and to myself).

In the year of leaving my marriage, a year of often being overwhelmed by rage (with time-outs to murmur loving-kindness incantations at Buddhist retreats), I began teaching a new course. I named it "Finding Peace". In the Buddhist tradition of loving-kindness meditation, we are asked to send sincere wishes for the happiness of oneself, a loved one, a mentor, a neutral person, and a difficult person. During this year I found it was helpful to use my ex-husband as my difficult person since it was clearly unproductive to wish bad things on the father of my children. My vindictive "small self" frequently bickered with my Higher Self: *Let him be lonely and miserable and regret that he didn't love me better—oh, damn, I'm supposed to love all sentient beings and I've already been making headway with the mosquitoes here.*

That practice and the journaling course I was giving did bring me some peace. I placed my attention on kindness. I found myself learning what I was teaching. I carried less anger. My shoulders descended half a centimeter.

Then I started teaching another course, "Writing on the Edge". Again I believed I was the very person to teach that course. I was daring, always had been since I was a tree-climbing toddler. At ten, a friend and I used to climb a seventy foot bridge that spanned a Toronto ravine, lunch bags held by our teeth. All my life I have put myself onto cliff edges, literal as well as metaphorical. I bagged my first high peak in the Adirondacks a few months after my ex-husband and I separated. As I stood 6,000 feet above the ground, wearing my green T-shirt with the word **WOMAN** celebrated in turquoise across my chest and grinning with elation, I felt I could take on *anything.*

However, until my fifties, I had never met an unbearable edge. So when, for the first time in my life, for no particular reason and with no warning, a large black crow came to sit on my shoulder every day at dusk, bringing blues I couldn't beat, what I had taught others helped me. I wrote about my feelings, allowed myself to truly feel. Through daily writing meditation, giving myself space and time in my journal, I pressed against a sharp ancient loneliness with my wide-nibbed fountain pen. I listened to myself. I remembered that everything passes.

As we write our journals, we revise our life scripts. The act of naming our feelings and our fears creates a chance to start to do things differently, to form a different way of relating than we were able to do before. We shape sentences to reshape ourselves.

If you are dating or considering dating, a journal can be your older sister, your friend, therapist, archivist, diviner, cartographer and comforter. It can be a midwife for creativity and compassion. It can be your Silver Fox stylist. Although a journal is a gift at any stage or time of life, the older you are the more life experience and wisdom you have to channel into your words.

I have been dating ever since I left my marriage. I have had many first dates, three long and a few shorter (around a year) relationships. I have also taken chosen breaks, a kind of serial celibacy, to recuperate and try to figure out what I was doing.

The analyzing and recuperating were mostly done by journaling. Yes, I've had therapy in these past nineteen years (feminist, gestalt, an hour of counseling from a nun who told me that I "had too much guilt"). I've meditated at Vipassana and Zen retreats, and dabbled in divination. All of these were helpful, but writing in a journal has been the best, cheapest, and most portable modality for rebalancing, learning and late-blooming.

Writing in a high-flying, free-flowing or self-reflective way has helped me figure out what I wanted, and what I didn't want. It helped me be a better teacher. It helped me become a Silver Fox. It can help you too.

As you journal, you are telling the story of your life and then retelling it. Each telling deepens your understanding of who you are. You might find yourself surprised at how differently you can see a situation from one decade to the next, one year to another, one day after the previous day. Your recounting the story and stories of your life often leads to change and wisdom. It always leads to this truth: your life is important.

As women who are growing older in an ageist society, we care about keeping our souls intact while searching for sexual love. I invite readers of this book to join with me in forming a virtual circle. As we write our lives, we can give ourselves the nuanced attention of a supportive listening circle. We can imagine being heard by a peer support group. As you read these words, know that there are thousands of women feeling the exact same longings, curiosity and trepidation—the same excitement and desire.

I have enjoyed dating during these past years, even though there has been some sadness and heartbreak. I've never been used, abused, or put-down as "too old". Writing helped me through difficult times, helped remove blocks to being comfortable with myself, and helped me to unlock my heart to others. Writing provided a map for risk-taking and adventure.

Writing helped me send out the vibes that attracted adoring men ready to fall at the flat feet of a sixty-something woman.

I'm hoping that my thoughts and samples from my journals will be helpful at this point in your life. I'm hoping—in typical older sister fashion—to give advice that you'll want to take.

If I can be belatedly popular, you can too. A spiral notebook with heavy white pages and a pen that fits your hand can be the beginning of a new relationship with yourself. Writing to revise your life can be the start of something big, a whole new affair with love, sexuality and yourself.

Do you have to keep a journal to profit from this book?

It's obvious that I strongly recommend keeping a journal. However, I know you may have reasons not to write at this moment. Perhaps you have never kept a diary. Or you've already tried to keep a journal and couldn't keep it up. Of course, you are welcome to simply read what interests you in this book. As well, there are other means of expressing yourself. You can relate your stories to a trusted friend, a therapist, to one of your groups, or to yourself as you are falling asleep or walking down the street. You can tell your tale through art, music or choreography.

You can daydream. Imagine that once upon a time there was a little girl who grew up denying and covering her problems and needs. Sound familiar? As she pursued her desire for love a struggle ensued. Now she is changing and understanding how she can up and leave her programmed story. She can fantasize an alternate story.

You can create a collage journal, expressing yourself in sketches, watercolours, by pasting ticket stubs, magazine photos, cut up pieces of love letters and other artifacts onto the pages. Even if you don't feel like writing, you might jot down brief notes and perceptions. Later, if you want to, you can use those random thoughts and insights as journaling prompts.

If you are willing to keep a dating diary, begin by buying a pen that writes smoothly and feels good in your hand. Buy a new notebook. I like the black sketch books you can buy at art supply stores, the ones bound with metal spirals. They are inexpensive, and can be personalized by adding a cover postcard or your own sketch. They also have quality blank paper on which you can write, paste mementos, and paint. You can give your notebook a title with intention: *Going Through a Hard Time with Grace, In Love and Learning* etc. And you can inscribe a quotation on the first page to send you on your way. I'm particularly fond of Doris Lessing's "Whatever you are meant to do, do it now. The conditions are always impossible."

And Paul Valery's "Une difficulté est une lumière/ Une difficulté insurmontable est un soleil." (A difficulty is a light / An insurmountable difficulty is the sun).

Start from stillness, either the natural stillness when first waking or just before falling asleep. If you are writing during the day, stop and breathe. Let go of attachment to grammar, spelling, or perfection. You don't have to be neat, you don't have to write well, you don't have to be nice, you don't have to censor, you don't have to think. You just have to write. Write ahead of your mind, out of your mind, what's on your mind.

Write for a few minutes, for a few pages, for a set time, or until you wear your thoughts out. Make threadbare thoughts you were attached to, thoughts you have become bored with, thoughts you have come to realize are only strands of your perceived truth at a certain time.

Here are two journaling catalysts, each followed by an excerpt from my own journals. (Some names and details have been changed in the journal pieces.)

Journal #1: *Getting Started: Begin your Dating Diary.*

(July, 2002) A new journal. I'm sitting on the couch in the living room, awash in sunlight and Mozart, drinking a second cup of coffee with foamed organic skim milk, and thinking of starting something with Michael, who sent the most interesting reply to my ad yesterday. Strangely, Peter also responded to my ad, obviously not realizing it was me he was writing to. I'm not going to answer Peter, even though he's lying heavy on my mind again. I'll email Michael and see what happens. Is it possible to love and still be free?

I'm happy, conscious of my luck to be at the beginning of "retirement", with interesting teaching jobs at two arts schools. Ten years ago I was single and pathetically grateful when couples invited me to a dinner party. I was honoured that someone like Peter would pay attention to me. Now, here I am, pushing sixty, finally comfortable in the world, with my future ahead of me.

Journal #2: *Write about a love that was difficult. Put yourself back in time and ask: What do I see? What do I want? What am I thinking? Feeling? Look over what you have written. What didn't you dare to say?*

(May, 1996) I asked myself if there was even one sexy man at that Council of Canadians meeting. Oh, god, yes.Yes. Anton, lecturing on genetic modification, taking my breath away. He looks like my father in his forties, like my grandfather in the sepia photos.

I was ready to fly; he is a friend to fly with.

Ecstasy is there between us. I'm not worried about how much he likes me. I know the connection.

He's teaching me how to make a space inside myself and listen when confronted. He's helping me know myself as a sexual creature.

But I'm scared to be diminished into a wife, scared to be loved for my use, not for me.

Silver Fox Tip

Begin writing to baroque music (I like Glenn Gould's rendition of the Goldberg Variations), with an inspiring drink (champagne, lavender tea?) at the ready.

We write to taste life twice. Colette

-2-
The Method Eclectic

○ ○

What happens with a teacher is not that he or she tells you what to do, but reveals who you are. Unknown lama

When I was ten, I vowed in my Nancy Drew diary (with its dark green cover and satisfying little lock and key) that I would not marry until I was twenty-five because I wanted to have adventures. I believed that all adventures ended once you became a wife.

In my early twenties, when I was fussing about whether to accept a marriage proposal or to learn Hebrew on a border kibbutz, I found that entry in my 1954 diary and it helped me leave Toronto and security for Israel and adventure.

Throughout my life, keeping a diary and dating have always been intertwined. I have recorded my relationships with guys since I was nine years old. The record shows a mixture of giddy happiness, guilt, heartache, and confusion. Not until I became a Crone (a woman who has reached the age of wisdom) did I feel that I had men and pen firmly in hand.

One of the advantages of journaling is that it allows you to keep documentation of felt sense. You can see, in your own handwriting, what you were actually feeling at a given time. Some years ago I wanted to go back to a romance I had left. I missed that lover terribly while on insipid first dates or when awakening from dreams of him. I was able to stay with my pain and resist quick false comfort because I could read my experience of feeling more anguish than ecstasy in that relationship. Of my seven journals kept during that love affair, few pages chronicled happiness; most revealed torment. I had repeatedly written things such as: "It's early in the morning and I'm filled with so much sadness."

But that sort of information can only be available when you let your writing take you to where you actually are. You can create documentation of your unedited feelings. If you are prepared to make your journal dangerous, if you are willing to let your writing tell you what you don't want to hear, don't want to deal with, you will sometimes surprise yourself. Hornets trapped in memory are stirred up and fly off the page.

If we sometimes feel powerless, hysterical, self-absorbed, all the better to vent on paper. If we journal, we can avoid acting out or dumping on our friends. By entering the silence between person and page, we allow ourselves the possibility of an expanding inner space.

A journal can also help us draft a blueprint of a world we want. It can support the forming of a better, truer, more effective self, especially if we need to reintegrate what the world has shattered. A journal can be a method of self-coaching, a conjuror of creativity, your daily meditation, your therapist or spiritual counselor, your dear friend, your to-do list, your Mother. You decide, and decide again each time, according to your need.

The approach to journaling that I have found most productive is sometimes called free writing, automatic writing, or timed writing. While keeping your pen moving, your hand begins writing you. It's not about the conscious noting of events or even feelings. It's about dipping into the ink of not-yet-accessible thought-forms, about invoking the stuff that dreams are made of. It's clutching your pen and, feet flying in the air behind you, following the black scratches on white paper until you reveal what you always knew but didn't know you knew, or what you didn't want to know but knew you knew. It's an adventure.

This kind of journaling is about letting go of conditioned thinking. If you write when you're falling asleep or are just waking, or just after you have been running or dancing or making art, your editing brain is usually switched off, your self-judgment on hold.

The method is not new. Writers such as the surrealists were doing it ages ago. So let's do it. Let's fall in love with our Silver Fox selves. Let's give ourselves time and space and kind attention.

After years of learning from other writers and teachers of writing, as well as from additional teachings (Buddhist, shamanic, psychological, life coaching etc.), I have developed my own teaching style. I call it "The Method Eclectic". I have borrowed, adapted, and created exercises which I will share with you in the following chapters, including: The Write (writing to learn your own mind), The Plan (from Lynda Barry via one of her college instructors), the unsent letter (written never to be sent), improv writing, poetry from a trigger, dialogue between parts of self, timed exercises, word painting, the monologue, and visualization. These techniques, and others, will help you imagine and script your wished-for future.

The act of journal-keeping while dating is helpful for immediate learning and rebalancing, and it has larger rewards. Many experience personal metamorphoses through keeping a journal, and the more emotional the material, the deeper the change. Dating certainly provides charged material. And deep writing transforms as well as releases energy.

Daily writing combined with mindful dating has become part of my meditation practice.

Once you know who you are and what you want, you will be far more capable of stepping out onto the dating dance floor with confidence. With the support of your journal and our "circle", you can become a person who foxtrots with pizzazz, able to venture into another's world without losing yourself.

Journal #3: *Write a creation myth (imagine the new you and how you came to be).*

(November, 1995) Elaina was born at the age of almost 50. Elaina is wilder than Elaine, and is truer to herself. She can climb mountains. She can tune into her needs and act on them. Because she became braver through hard passages, Elaina is not as manipulable as Elaine was – she has a strong centre. She is a good friend and partner. She'll succeed at whatever she wants to.

She is leaving tracks in the world with a fire-tailed pen, dipped in her own blood, the fire never consuming the paper, the blood-letting never hurting her. She is hoping others will want to follow those tracks, hoping it can help them find their way.

Silver Fox Tip

Be eclectic! Take whatever you wish from each chapter, write only if you want to, use other modes of exploration, or just read this book. You'll retain what you need.

...expressing feeling is directly linked with creation. My telling all to the diary helped me in this... Anais Nin

- 3-
Your Life as Story

○ ○

All suffering is bearable if it seen as part of a story.

Isak Dinesen

How do we discover our Silver Fox selves?

Jung said that pathology comes from stories untold. As journalers, we tell and retell the stories of our lives. We become our own allies, searching for clues to the mystery of who we are. We choose to seek out what we have hidden from ourselves through denial and in unconsciousness. As detectives, we document what we are doing and why we are doing it, moment by moment. We let this evidence lead us to buried information. And we allow ourselves to hear that information.

We not only need to listen to our own stories, we need to be heard. Many friends, lovers, my sister, my children, at times my parents, and two therapists have listened me into understanding, into "oh, yes, I get it" perceptions. If our stories are heard with understanding, we can be listened into being our real selves.

Sometimes we tell our tales to comfort, sometimes to connect, or to amuse, and just to say, "this is who I am, this is my life." Often we write or tell stories to make ourselves look good, justify something, bring a listener or reader to tears or laughter, explain why we have difficulty with something, or relate how we overcame an impossible obstacle. When applying

15

for a job, reassuring mother, or impressing an attractive new guy, we are aware of which of our stories to relate to present the best image. Our stories are fueled by our agendas.

We know that it's important to reveal something of ourselves even though we sometimes hide behind deliberate fiction or through careful editing. We are often ashamed to expose what we believe are unacceptable parts of our lives. Yet there's a need to have our truths heard by others. In telling our stories, we are saying that we matter, that the details of our lives are significant, that who we are as human beings and as women, counts. In the telling, we are also creating who we are. If we study our own and each other's stories, we can learn how to live and love more freely.

When a self-contained friend disclosed that she was thinking of leaving her husband, I was shocked. As she told me her dissatisfactions without shame, or second-guessing, or her usual relentless fairness, I heard her clearly, and began to acknowledge my own fearful thoughts of leaving my marriage.

Most women I know had a best friend in adolescence with whom they talked and talked, the talk acting as a chrysalis for emerging into teen life. My best friend and I even created a language so that we could talk about boys in secret. With a journal as your new "best friend", you can listen to yourself as you tell your stories over and over, stories that often become more nuanced, more layered, and more sophisticated at each telling. In doing this work it will be important for you to recognize what your stories reveal. Are you stuck on one theme? Have you been focusing on negative readings of your life's happenings? Can you find the patterns in your storytelling? Allowing yourself to transform into a Silver Fox means allowing yourself to tell new stories about your own desirability, sweetness and sexiness.

There is often a tension between truth and fiction, depending on mood, memory, and self-editing, so there is usually room to choose a vision of who we are at any moment. It makes sense that we might as well put a positive spin on what we tell ourselves about who we are. We also have a take on all the other "characters" in our stories, the major and the minor ones, and we could choose to see them positively as well. To some extent, we construct and reconstruct all the *dramatis personae* in the told and retold tales of our lives.

My character, "Elaine", is hardly perfect, but perhaps she's wonderful. It's a balancing act, remembering as I write that I am both uncovering my truest self and also portraying myself as the protagonist. I do my best to love the central character—me—while telling the truth!

With practice, we can hold paradox along with our pens.

As well as benefitting from hearing ourselves and from the individuals who hear us, we gain confidence from an understanding group. We all want to be seen with friendly eyes for who we actually are. We want to be able to tear off our confining masks. We need the support of others to become our own cheerleaders.

There are closed circles and open circles. The closed ones rope us into conformity, insist we cut off parts of ourselves to fit into the rigid mold. Many women remember the high school clique—constricting to be inside one, miserable to be shunned.

Luckily, the journaling groups that I teach have all been supportive circles. The merest whiff of judgment could have caused any of us to close up. But it's never happened. Such circles nourish individuality and originality. They allow each to speak her truth, to cry, to show anger, to lower protective shields. Some women have announced that they have never before told *anyone* a closeted revelation; others have declared that the journaling circle was better than any therapy.

Most of us have at least one circle of women, a circle that feels safe and gives us power and inspiration. Whether it's a knitting or quilting group, a writing circle, an underground energy circle, a *Sex-in-the*-City group that giggles over *Cosmopolitans*, or a political group, these circles can be flexible and strong. They are in plain sight, yet holding the potential to be subversive to the balance of gender power.

My circles include occasional dinners with far-flung high school friends, annual meals with university pals, friends from an Orthodox Jewish school where I worked more than thirty years ago, old friends from married days, the continuing connection of many colleagues and students from my twenty-five years working at City Alternative High School in Toronto, as well as the women from journaling groups I lead, and the women of my father's family.

Ask for help from your women's groups. Allow yourself to be supported by positive people. Be specific about how others can help you. For example, you could ask if anyone knows a terrific single man, a good gynecologist, or a great masseuse.

It might also help to visualize a very open circle comprised of women who are using this book. We are not alone as we reach for a better life, as we open ourselves up to the best love (and the best sex) of our lives. We are working towards a common goal. The more we risk for ourselves, the more we create space for other women to risk.

You are in good company.

Once, when I was at a workshop in upstate New York, I met Nora, a beautiful and charming woman who was both a Harvard trained therapist and a Celtic shaman. She told me of her concept of "The Woman at the Head of the Table", an Alpha female who co-ordinates our many selves.

Imagine that your Head Woman is looking around the boardroom table at all your other selves. Do you have a Power Woman? What does she look like? Is there a totem animal with her? What gift does she bring you? Is your I've-Got-to-Have-it-Now Gal at the table? Studious Serena? The Lioness? Your own private Greta Garbo? Does your Inner Critic nag as much as your mom did? Is Wild Woman teasing Nervous Neurotica? Is the Lady who's a Tramp comforting your inner toddler? And who is the Unknown Woman – do you want to get to know her? All our selves bring gifts and difficulties to the table.

Sometimes it is useful to call a meeting to explore an issue, say, how to have a difficult conversation with a man. In this kind of meeting, I envision the Woman at the Head of the Table preparing to make an executive decision. It might take quite a while before she's able to decide among the competing voices, but when she has spoken, all my selves (that I know of) have been heard.

There are many reasons to write your stories. You might want to have raw material for memoir or fiction and to gain practice in writing. You might want to make sense of your life, by synthesizing the past and writing a new script for the future. You could be writing to find out what you already know. You might scribble your way out of a stuck situation. The strongest motivation for using pen and paper could be to prepare yourself to love and be loved.

Writing a journal means that, facing your ocean, you are afraid to swim across it, so you attempt to drink it drop by drop.

George Sand

Journal #4: *Who am I? "Ask" someone (grandmother, parent, child, friend) who you are. Write an imagined reply.*

(October, 1995) Who am I? According to whom? To my sister, compulsively neat, to my ex-husband, a slob. My daughter thinks I'm Anxiety Incarnate, my son sees me as balanced. One friend tells me I'm too picky with men, another holds me as a shining example of a woman who won't settle for less than she believes she deserves. One of my nieces told me I was controlling, her sister turns to me because she finds me open and non-judgmental. According to me, depending on the day you ask me, I might be fattish or wired or difficult. On another day, I can adore myself and be easy in the world. According to my mother, I was supportive, kind, never held a grudge, and she could depend on me to be real with her. According to my Mother-with-Alzheimer's, I was a bitch who was infantilizing her and could never do enough for her. Who knows who I am?

Journal #5: *Ask yourself, "What have I been telling myself by writing my story in my journal?"*

(December 1993) Through rereading my journals, I am understanding that I want to live alone and have a love that is convenient, on my terms, in my bed when I wish it, and not underfoot. I'm scared of my love for Peter. I doubt it will bring me happiness. I have been passive and now I want to be more of a player in my own life. I hope that if I keep writing about what I am really feeling I will be able to hear myself, and be strong enough to do whatever I believe is the right thing. I see that I'm hooked on the kind of stuff that only increases my anxiety. Caffeine, empty carbohydrates, and wine and romance. All those detailed descriptions of the perfect coffee, the perfect croissant, the glass of grand cru, the perfect lover. I seem to be obsessed with what I believe makes up *la bonne vie* .

Just one cup of coffee a day, sweetie, and only have good dark chocolate (70%). Only three desserts a week. While you're at it, no boasting, no leaning on others. And stop trying to drive muscles, to drive sensations. Stop trying to drive other people. Stop acting like a Type A train. Do the *jinsendo* exercises, some yoga, and the "rites" every day (those exercises that will keep you forever young). Meditate. Greet each day. Don't chase after every new thing. Say NO without explanation.

Silver Fox Tip

If you are worried that someone will read your words without permission, you could secrete completed journals in a safety deposit box. Conceal a present journal in a locked chest, or in the trunk of your car. Hide it in plain sight, as in Poe's short story, "The Purloined Letter". Or keep your diary inside a hollowed out book, a board game box, hat box, a cookbook cover, or a flour canister.

Your life expands or contracts according to your courage

Anais Nin

-4-
Mom and Dad and all that...

○ ○

Whence come I? I come from my childhood. I come from my childhood as from a homeland. Antoine de Saint-Exupery

Every morning the painterly light entered my *casita* like hope. But on the round glass table, my laptop and the seventeenth draft of my first novel lay like dead fish. I would stare at the peach adobe fireplace, tourmaline marble floor, carved and cushioned furniture. If I turned to gaze at my private patio, caramel clay tiles and scarlet bougainvilleas, the hummingbird was usually balancing on the blue-tiled sundial, singing her advice.

Across the lane from my small turquoise rental, I practiced very slow yoga in the San Miguel Meditation Centre, trying to stay in the now.

Will I have to look after my mother for the next ten years?

I was blocked. Not as blocked as my mother, whose mind had taken a turn to oblivion. I had become my mother's keeper. Her advocate, caregiver, victim.

How could you leave your mother at a time like this?

The courtyard of the Santa Monica Hotel offered respite, of a kind. Hot sun, a stone fountain, more bougainvilleas, and a frozen margarita. But the laughing tourists were all in pairs.

22

Will I ever find love?

I was a runaway before I was five. In the late forties in Toronto, I followed the icemen and their horses, followed parades, chased a cute little white dog. When I got the tricycle I longed for, the one I slept with my arms around in my fourth year, I knew I could go farther. Wheels!

As soon as I started kindergarten, I began to hang out at friends' houses. Then their cottages in the summers. After school and on the weekends I got away by skating, hiking, biking, playing tennis, taking ballet and piano lessons, playing dress-up, and directing plays. When I wasn't with my friends, I was reading, always with my "nose in a book", even at the dinner table, another fine means of escape. And when I wasn't reading, I was writing novels, all imitations of *Anne of Green Gables,* all starring smart feisty orphan girls.

I often walked over to the *biblioteca,* the bilingual library and cultural centre, to borrow books or to see a film such as the one on Mexican migrant workers in upstate New York. Usually, I came and left alone, conscious that others were part of either a group or a couple. But after that film, three single women of about my age asked me to join them for a drink on *Calle Jesus.* Another courtyard, another fountain, caged yellow birds, and my companions analyzing their mothers while I kept silent and downed two margaritas.

Unremittingly sweet to the rest of the world, my mother used me as a repository for her unowned depression and anger. Although I taught her to treat me with respect when I left home at twenty-one, the controls came off when she was almost ninety. The abuse was terrible and familiar, but I was the "good" daughter, the daughter in town, the daughter who had to look after her.

The first time I lived abroad, it was to get away from both mother *and* father. When I was twenty, my immigrant father forbade me to move out (*only whores leave a nice Jewish home for an apartment in the same city*). In 1966, a Canadian could teach in England with just an undergraduate degree, so I sailed away. I was desperate to grow up, and an ocean seemed the best protection from parental overprotection.

I did grow up. A little.

After I returned from England, I moved to my own apartment. For the better part of a year, my father told everyone who called me at their home that I "had just stepped out for a moment".

When I was ten, I wrote, "I will not marry until I am twenty-five because once you get married all adventures stop and you have to serve supper a lot." I was twenty-three when I left my parents and three suitors for Israel and adventure. I learned "easy Hebrew", taught English to diplomats and pop stars, made good friends, edited a book by a former Israeli chess champion, worked on a border *kibbutz* where we were shelled every night, and went to political soirees with my boyfriend who was Shimon Peres' speech writer. I returned home more grown up and ready for marriage.

I married. Two children. Divorced. (I wasn't all that ready for marriage.)

That January in San Miguel, I took Spanish lessons at the *Instituto*. Only one hour a day, baby Spanish, but I loved being a student again. As well as the Tuesday and Thursday slow yoga, on other mornings I took rigorous yoga classes at *Bellas Artes*. After class I sometimes went with yoga pals to another charming courtyard, and a breakfast of chopped mango, eggs and bacon, toast and coffee with hot foamed milk, yet I still felt lonely. The other women were all town residents, all close friends, and I knew they included me out of kindness.

After my marriage ended, what I most loved about my long distance relationship with a man from Massachusetts (besides the man) was the freedom of the road. I sang in the car as I left

Toronto and all the post-marriage difficulties, and I sang as I left the Berkshires for eight hours on the road again.

Always fearful of being trapped, I've looked for alternative worlds. In the years after my marriage ended, road trips with my teenage children, Buddhist retreats, work exchanges, a gig teaching writing in the far north of British Columbia—all these gave me more life, the way lucid dreaming gives you a night country as well as your everyday one, the way writing a novel gives you a larger world. I needed all that space, even though my mother and I were getting along well enough and my father (having apologized in a Polish Jewish accent for his sexism) was becoming my great friend and ally.

And then my father died. I made the moral choice to phone my mother every day and saw her often. She expected much more, let me know that good daughters visited parents at her condominium complex *every day*.

All my mother's friends: *You're so lucky to have such a lovely mother.*

Two weeks after I arrived in San Miguel, I fell into joining and sometimes leading a writing workshop at the Aristo Hotel with Kathleen and her group of kick-ass Texas women. They all looked like ladies and what a grand camouflage that was. They wrote like wild women and I followed, making black scratches on white paper until I revealed what I didn't want to know. I had unleashed my inner Silver Fox, and lustful and murderous imaginings ran unchecked. Half way through my month away, I could write again.

Ten years after my father's death, I saw an ad for an English teacher at Neuchatel Junior College, a private Canadian school in Switzerland. I was so clear about wanting that job that I bought an expensive traditional gray suit (had been wearing jeans to my lefty alternative school for fifteen years) for my interview. In another country, in a town that Alexandre Dumas described as "a toytown carved out of butter", I realized that my clarity had been sharpened by the ongoing desire to get away from mother. I had a year of living in an apartment right out of a Jeanne Moreau film, a year of delighting in the town, the job, *jura* cheese, local *pinot gris*, artisanal chocolate, most everyone I met, the travel, *tout.* A lifelong insomniac, I slept so well in Neuchatel.

I returned home to a hot polluted city and a mother who had been diagnosed with Alzheimer's while I was away. My younger sister, who lived in Thunder Bay, had been flying in to organize necessities, but now the Designated Daughter was back. Most people remember the lyrical loving of food in the film, *Like Water for Chocolate*. I remember the voracious mother and the doomed first-born daughter.

Did my mother ever care about me as a separate person? An early memory, which she later validated, was when I dropped her hand to explore a park at the age of three, and she freaked out. She had been abandoned by the early death of her mother, and continually let me know I was a bad, selfish "cold potato" if I weren't attending to her needs. So began my guilt. So began my travelling.

All my aunts and uncles: *You have to be good to your mother.*

I wrote in the early afternoons at the glass table, belting out "I Wish I Were in Love Again" or "Don't Fence Me In", with the hummingbird as backup.

I started going to the frequent gallery openings—excellent art, margaritas, sometimes folk music against a background of church bells. And interesting people—everyone in San Miguel (sometimes described as a college town for the young older crowd) was excited about learning something: sculpture, dance, watercolour painting, Spanish, weaving. Dinner invitations were proffered by new friends.

In the late afternoons, I hung out with my hummingbird, and repeatedly asked for my heart to open to my mother. I did it for her, and I did it for me. I was single, sixty, and believed I wouldn't find a partner for the last stage of my life as long as I was clutched by her desperation and my resentment.

I knew I wanted love. One morning I walked along dusty roads to the old church of San Antonio de la Casa and prayed to San Antonio to find a mate. Dropped 13 coins in his box as a "sincere deposit" or earnest money and gave some coins to an old lady who helped me. She blessed me and gave me a stale bun.

You don't have to be nice, sang the tiny green bird after I returned to my *casita*, threw out the bun and made myself a margarita.

I'm not so nice anymore. I've learned to honour my feelings.

I was caring for a woman who was abusing me in exactly the same way she did when I was little. I couldn't leave her then; I couldn't leave her when she was ill. I had made a vow that I would never abandon her. At the same time, I vowed that I would never abandon myself. I told my mother (who had some emotional understanding), "You have to stop treating me badly." She responded by shrieking, "You do nothing for me, *nothing.*" Eventually, she was more careful with me, for a while. "I know I have to be nice," she confided.

Although I visited often and worked hard to keep her in her own place where she still had a life and some happiness, I asked my sister to take over more and hired a kind woman and various others to look after mother's physical needs. I looked after myself in other ways too. Therapy, dance classes, reflexology, acupuncture not only helped me get through the relentless days and nights, they helped me grow up a little more.

At dusk, everyone gathered in the *Jardin*, the central square. Towards the end of my retreat month, I sat on a bench under a large breadfruit tree, and was blessed with an unexpected visit of equanimity as I listened to the mariachi bands, and watched the courting couples, ice-cream vendors, and children playing in front of the strange landmark church, the pink *Perroquia*. Because I was not choked by duty, compassion for my mother unfolded and expanded inside me.

So far from Toronto, I realized that it wasn't only a distant location that gave freedom from a difficult parent. My mother's heartbreaking disease, and the terrible level of demand on me, had forced me to build better boundaries. On Mexican time, I could appreciate the many ways my mother supported me. She not only drove me crazy and away, she gave me gifts of adoration and money, believed I could do anything (except give her enough love), backed me in whatever I decided to do, and inspired me by the amount of adventuring she did in a limited life. I can see that she gave me much more than she was given by her mother, a hard thing to do.

You have to know how to love 'em, and how to leave the enmeshment. Surely sixty was past time to separate from a wonderful and terrible mother. The real getaway was in my mind. Something hard had become soft. I could love my mother, just as she was. And something soft—my spine—had become strong.

You don't have to be so good, my patio hummingbird scatted her refrain. I blew her a kiss.

Two days before I leave Mexico, while waiting for a Hollywood musical to begin at Hotel Villa Jacaranda, I met Andy. He walked into the lobby with his brother. They told me that the first part of the movie was filmed in San Miguel. His brother went upstairs to see the Mario Lanza potboiler. Andy stayed fixed, and then sauntered towards me. We began our dialogue in the lobby and ended up at a nearby restaurant rooftop, eating *chiles en nogada* in the setting sun, and talking until we closed the place down.

Since my mother died, my relationship with her keeps getting better. I miss her, especially as she was in the forty years we enjoyed each other. I keep picturing her in the fuzzy pink hat I bought her in Mexico, the hat she wore every time she was out on the porch of the nursing home.

Dad is another story. Although I got along with him very well, liked and loved him, I cut my father off from full emotional connection for much of my adult life. He was wonderful—decent, funny, smart, kind, supportive of family, friends, and strangers—but at some point I made the assumption that I could never completely reach him, that he would never be able to hear me. He did hear me when he was dying, when I was able to say things that were hard for me to say, that had felt impossible to say, and they turned out not to be so hard, and he listened extraordinarily well. I realized that I had left men, or cut them off, rather than say the hard things, the things I thought I couldn't say.

Some years ago, I had a dream about my dad. He was a naked baby, sheltered by my heart. He wasn't clinging to me. The ventricles of my heart were clutching him. I pulled him out, gently but forcibly, and my heart was bruised. I gave him to the goddess Sophia for mothering. When I woke up I began to question my compulsive tendency to mother the men in my life.

My relationship with my father also improves with time. I'm proud of what he accomplished in his life, of the conscious and brave way he died. He loved and protected me, our family, and many others. I miss him. I don't idealize him but I wish I could see him again, be able to tell him things, share the kind of humour we had between us.

Mom and dad and all that… We learned from them how to relate to a loved one, or how to be a "loved" one. Family relationships can be nourishing and difficult. Both healthy and distressing patterns can repeat themselves in other relationships throughout our lives, and the distressing ones will continue to be acted out on automatic pilot unless we become conscious of them. When we become more aware, we can see how we hurt our children. We can know when we are unkind to others.

What are your family patterns? The marital relationships in my family were characterized by strong, stoical, martyrish women and men who were somewhat "out of it". As a family, our strengths were that we were grounded, responsible, decent in the community, generous, kind, financially stable, healthy, fun and we looked after each other. The rules were: be nice to everyone, don't make waves, don't be too trusting, and don't blab about family dirty laundry. The beliefs that I carry from my family are that the world is interesting, having enough money matters to have a good life, you should be there when people need you, and *always* give when asked.

I find that I have a desperate need to keep writing to free myself from family conditioning. One device I use is to create wise inner parents. I imagine what advice I would give myself if I were my ideal mother or father. When I mother myself and others I am nurturing. When I father myself, I don't take crap, and I have good boundaries.

Whether the patterns were woven with us by our parents, by school, society, our friends, relatives or others, we all repeat some behaviours that limit our potential for true intimacy, and are generally not good for us or for other people. Once we recognize the weave, see the motifs in the fabric of our lives, we can create new patterns. We can do it in various ways: by listening to intimate others who let us know we are hurting them; through therapy; by taking on the challenges of travel or work or caregiving; by way of peer support groups, meditation and reading, and through writing our lives to understand how our family patterns are affecting our present relationships.

We don't have to feel pressure to change anything. By consciously observing, we will find that change happens.

Journal #6: Write an "unsent letter" (a letter never meant to be sent) to your mother and your father.

(To mother, 2002) When you yelled at me I felt that you were out of control and that I couldn't count on you. I never knew when you would blow up. Felt assaulted and furious. Then guilty because I didn't like you. Sometimes I loved you. Sometimes I needed you. You could give to me when I was really down. All those pretty Rosenthal cups of tea and sympathy. But when I was okay and you didn't feel needed, you were cruel to me.

P.S. When I reread my childhood diaries, you didn't yell as much as I remembered.

(To father, 1991) Dad, when you didn't acknowledge my feelings or give me credit for achievement, I don't remember feeling hurt. I would laugh at your one-upmanship and find you cute. Sometimes I was frustrated by you but mostly I just kept trying to reach you.

Journal #7: Write to your forebears, telling them how you intend to do things differently.

(Summer, 1999) Aunty Tany, at 94 you are almost blind, living your own senior's apartment, and crocheting scarves which are sold in the Baycrest Shop to raise money for the building. And mom, at 84 arthritis and loneliness are a big part of your life, but you minister to your sick brother-in-law Harry, and play the piano every day. You feel that you are progressing in your playing.

I stand on your shoulders, and I'm grateful that you "girls" were from a family of survivors on both sides. But at the same time I recognize that there was often not enough love, or security, or time, or room to fulfill yourselves. Yet you had energy and creativity. I have followed your tradition of working hard and competently and keeping going, no matter what.

Now I want to continue breaking some of our family's negative behaviours, such as either being too compliant, or yelling at people I care about when really all I want to do is to lessen my own anxiety. If I can make some of these shifts, I'll be better able to love myself and a man.

Journal #8: *Write a poem or a monologue from the point of view of someone with whom you are having difficulty or unfinished business. Try to recreate the voice of that person.*

Monologue from Father

I'm your father, Elaine, remember, I know you. You're so adorable, so smart. I'm proud of you, *Elainella,* and you're beautiful too, but tell me, why do you get so angry? Why make mountains out of mole heads? Why don't you just relax and let your old dad take care of things. You don't have to worry (not like I did in Poland without a father)—you'll get everything you need. You're the best but where did that 5% on the test go, why only 95? No nice boy will marry you if you wear those bohemian clothes and move out of the house and travel away from us and swear and say whatever you like. You make me laugh and you ease my depression (what are you talking about, you're 100% wrong, I'm tough I'm strong I have no depression). Why won't you do as I say?

Poem from Mother

What does she want from me?
Maybe to tear out my heart
I tried to be such a good mother
I never said no to her I gave her so much
love I never got enough
love from my mother
She always wanted to get away from me
She hurt me terribly
I did everything for her
Elaine is such a lucky little girl
She's such a miserable *nishuma*
A wild thing, a wonderful daughter
She loves her children more
than she loves me
I want her to have everything
I love her more than life itself

Silver Fox Tip

*Frimmi's motto about life – **Slurp it up!***

(*Frimmi* was my mom's name. It was a form of *Fruma*, which means "religious" in Yiddish.)

The family – that dear octopus from whose tentacles we never quite escape, nor, in our inmost hearts, ever quite wish to.

Dodie Smith

-5-

Intentions

○ ○

Neurosis "is a disease of the attention." Gertrude Stein

To date well, it is important to have clear goals. If you don't know what you are looking for in a man, you might accept anyone with a pulse. You might put up with bad boys with bad behaviour. Or resign yourself to a man who is almost but not quite "the one".

Once you begin to know yourself and to know what you want, you can save a lot of time by avoiding men who are wrong for you, or not interesting enough, or who want something other than what you want in life. Once you are clear, you will be able to give your time, energy, and body to the right man. You will give what you can give, and only when you wish to.

Energy can flow if the birth passage of your desire is clear and unambiguous. The intention can be manifested. However, if the passage is blocked by ambivalence, then the desire could be stillborn.

In other words, we obstruct desires by our fears and mixed feelings. We stay with lovers longer than is beneficial for us. We push away good men. We act out instead of asking for what we want. We end up running away from love that might have worked.

Don't worry about how you'll bring about your intention. Just be clear about what you want. If you want a wonderful love, it has a good chance to unfold as you naturally choose what will bring you nearer and ignore or avoid what will lead you away from it.

You could begin the process of clarification by making an inventory of all the things you want in a man. Catalogue five non-negotiable traits that you demand in a lover. Both lists helped me to become ready to receive a man with the key qualities. Eventually I reduced my list to these two attributes: passion and presence. As well, I have one emotional benchmark: Do I miss him? (Even when in a relationship, I have not missed most of the men I have "somewhat loved", but I have missed the few I've really loved.)

Intentions can be splintered. An example in my life was my desire to be with Peter, the first of my post-marriage loves, and my semiconscious desire to sabotage the relationship. I was confused at the time, a strange time, the crazy time right after my marriage ended. I was jumpy. I had no focus. I caused unintended pain for both Peter and myself.

An interesting study was done at Harvard concerning goal setting. In 1979, students in the Harvard MBA program were asked if they had set clear goals for the future. No goals at all were reported by 84% of them, 13% had goals but had not put them on paper, and 3% wrote down their goals. Twenty years later, in that longitudinal study, the 13% who had unwritten goals earned twice as much as the 84% with no goals. The 3% who wrote down goals earned ten times as much as the other 97% combined. The only difference among the groups was the clarity of their goals. While such a study may not translate perfectly into dating practices and finding love, it does speak to the potential importance of writing down our goals. Even if you aren't the kind of person who usually creates five year plans, if you act like a goal-oriented woman, you are more likely to realize your dreams. Allowing yourself to focus in this way, articulating and recording your desires, may be exactly what you need in order to find the love you want.

It is interesting to look at not just what you want, but why you want it. And you could go deeper—why do you want *that?* Or deeper still—what are your core beliefs or issues? If you can uncover a core belief such as my once unconscious idea that I was a bad person if I ate sweets, you can modify or change self-destructive behavior.

My recent decision to break my addiction to sugar began with this memory: I am eleven years old, sitting in my tiny bedroom closet, skirts and jeans dangling around my head, quickly stuffing down an Aero bar so that my mother (The Health Food Nut) won't see me and start yelling.

As I write this, I am a croissant-curved sixty-something who knows all the patisseries in downtown Toronto. I know where they are, what they specialize in, what I love most in each one.

When I was sixteen and most bakeries in Toronto were British, I was delighted to get a summer job at Hunt's Bakery. I wanted the money, but more, I wanted to get over my lust for sweets. Because we could eat anything and as much as we wanted from the store, I was sure that could happen. It didn't. I formed an even tighter relationship with trifle and eccles buns.

I have spent so many years in an internal struggle with the demon sugar. Even before I travelled to and then lived in Europe, I struggled with the expansive desire to enjoy the pleasures in life symbolized by *profiteroles* and *ile flottante* (yes, Paris) pitted against the narrowing belief that I shouldn't indulge myself. When I was growing up and slim, pimples were the outward symptom of my badness (according to the wisdom of the time and my mom). In the last twenty years it's been fat, just enough fat to render me non-glam.

I have tried to break free from my sugar habit: drinking eight glasses of water a day; putting my fork down between each thoroughly chewed bite; hypnotherapy ("imagine green worms slithering out of your favourite truffle..."); the ten day sugar fast; the leek soup that helps French women not get fat; "bibliotherapy" (I learned from books that the best diet is a diet from negativity, and also that I'm a victim, a feminist victim, of our crazy North American culture). For a brief period in the 90s, I countered negativity and victimhood by inviting the Divine Spirit to dine and binge with me, in the hope that my Higher Self might remember her manners.

I finally understood that I was not in control of my compulsion when I was working in French Switzerland, and found myself standing in front of every *patisserie* and every *chocolaterie*—**every day**—on the way to and from the school where I taught, each time wrestling with one of my selves (the Food Bully/ mommy!). Her—our—voice said, "That *tarte tatin* is just like heroin, and you're pathetic." My more indulgent voice argued back, "Here you are in Europe, the mother-ship, you've only had one very *petit pain au chocolat* for breakfast...and someday you're going to die."

When will I come out of that childhood closet and eat and love without fear? I want to be liberated from my continuing conflict, be able to weave flowers through the black hole of sadness or loneliness, rather than try to fill it with things made of flour. I fear becoming a baguette lady.

I hope I have finally begun to get over my obsession. With the help of a friend who is a cognitive therapist, I discovered the "hot thought" of that child gorging chocolate among the hanging clothes. With her assistance, I understood the core belief at the root of my acting out: *I am bad when I eat sweets.* Lately, I have substituted the hot thought with a replacement thought: *I am only bad when I eat sweets if I am not paying*

attention to the pleasure of the moment. In other words, if I am not grateful for the miracle of a great dessert.

Can I become slimmer, less matronly-looking, truly *une femme d'un certain age?* Can I be grateful for the miracle of a great man? Will I be able to pay attention to the pleasure of the moment without my usual disaster thinking?

These days I have made a vow to free myself from the sweet chains of addiction.

It is one part of a larger shift into becoming a woman of intention.

There are techniques for blossoming into just such a woman. Start with giving your new journal a title of purpose, for example, *Coming out of the Chocolate Closet, The Summer of My Brilliant Transformation, In Love and Learning, or Forget Fear!* Write every day for a month. If the idea of writing every day of a month seems like too much of a commitment, consider writing every day for a week to see how it feels. A writing ritual is a way to meditate, to give rhythm to your day, to acquire discipline, and to work towards clarifying goals and intentions.

If you write a sentence declaring the same intention every morning, for a set number of days (say 7, 11, 21 days), you will notice the strengthening of your purpose. If your goal is to be available for meeting and dating new men, you might write for the chosen number of days: "I will not refuse any offers to meet a man unless I sense danger or complete impossibility." Something will happen.

Manifestation can be defined as a co-creation between the energy in us and the energy in the world. It is a process that can bring to us what we want or need when the methods we normally use are not working. Manifestation works in unexpected, even seemingly magical ways. Things happen because we are receptive to them. If we concentrate, focus, think big enough, eliminate negative thoughts as they come up, and let go of attachment to the end result, miracles happen. When we see an open door, we walk through it instead of passing it by. What might otherwise seem coincidental becomes part of a happy story.

Imagine your heart's desire. If you are wishing for true love, using the principles of manifestation, you would first clear yourself of blocks such as ambivalence, anger or despairing thoughts of your age and chances. Whether or not you fully believe in the power of this process, be unambiguous about what you want. Listen to the guidance of your inner voice. You will begin to eliminate what and who doesn't work for you almost without conscious effort.

Even if you don't yet have what you want in love and in life, it's possible to send out an intention to be happy and surely happiness is a love magnet. Every morning I greet the day consciously and gratefully. I do a series of meditative, stretching, and aerobic exercises. One of the exercises is to turn to each of the four directions, starting with the east, circling my torso from my tailbone three times, while saying "Good morning" to each direction.

If you're single, choose to be happy whether resigned or searching. If you're stuck in a difficult or lifeless relationship, you could begin to become ready to make changes or leave. If you have a goal to have a man in your life, enjoy all that you can in present time as well as envisioning who and what you want. Date as often as you can (yes, endure boredom and disappointment), because if you're actively dating, the pheromones are signaling.

One of the best kept secrets I know is that if you want to be happy then…be happy. Sufi seer Pir Vilayet Khan says that there is only one relevant spiritual question: "Why aren't you dancing with joy at this very moment?"

There are only two ways to live your life. One is as though nothing is a miracle. The other is as though everything is a miracle. Einstein

Journal #9: Write a letter to yourself a year from now and ask yourself, "If anything were possible, what would I like to see happen in my love life?" Writing this letter will clarify your goals and give them form.

(April, 2004) Dear Elaine, If anything were possible I would have a juicy love, one in which we would have fun together, and keep wanting to touch each other. We would honour each other's hurt places and help with each other's healing. We would create a love that allows and encourages us to be our whole selves. We would simply relate to each other instead of figuring out what we have to do to, in my mother's words, "keep the relationship good." If anything were possible, I would finally be able to be the person who loves without constant vigilance, and whose lover doesn't have to "walk on eggshells" (as past lovers have reported feeling that they needed to do with me).

Silver Fox Tip

*Have the intention (and immediately begin) to live well, to enjoy whatever you think of as the good life, **la bonne vie**. Start now. **Sante!***

I learned this, at least, by my experiment; that if one advances confidently in the direction of his dreams, and endeavours to live the life he has imagined, he will meet with a success unexpected in common hours…If you have built castles in the air, your work need not be lost. That is where they should be. Now put the foundations under them. Henry David Thoreau

- 6 -
Writing from a Dream

○ ○

There is the whole mystery of growth, of expansion, of deliverance from the traps which life sets us, because life loves the drama of entrapping us and seeing whether we can get out. It's a game, a game of magic. Every difficult situation into which you are sometimes thrown has some kind of opening somewhere, even if it is only by way of the dream.

Anais Nin, *A Woman Speaks*

During my childhood, I kept having a nightmare in which my home city of Toronto was a war zone, my little sister and I were orphans, and I had to save her by leading her by the hand as we crawled along telephone wires above the bombed city streets.

What interests me most about dreams is the stories we make out of them. Different experts or amateurs might pronounce on what a given image signifies, but the fabric the dreamer spins out of the dream threads is what holds meaning for me. It is the dreamer's story—not the dream—that carries the message that matters.

My recurring nightmare told me my truth—not *the* truth— that when I was a child I felt like an orphan, that I thought I had to take care of myself and also rescue others. I asked myself how that core belief affected my choices in men. I looked at how I set up my intermittent feeling of aloneness.

A dream can inspire and inform creative writing. Many novelists and poets have told of works hatched from dreams. I sometimes ask my dream-maker for specific help with one of the mystery stories I write. Just as I'm falling asleep, I might say, "I'd like to know how to make a transition between the heroine's B&E and the romantic sub-plot". At a time when my ex-husband and I were selling a house, our difficulties were exacerbated by a sleazy real estate agent. A dream image, the agent's corpse lying in front of that house, the sold sign staked through his body into the summer grass, triggered a prize-winning story.

I keep a notebook and pen on my night table (one of those pens with a light in it in case I am sleeping with someone else), and I write what I can recall of the dream. I ask: "What do I see? Who are the people in the dream? What are the sounds, smells, tastes, textures, colours? Are there objects that intrigue me? How does the dream make me feel? Is there a question this dream is raising?"

I started asking for help from the night country when I was a teenager. Throughout my life, when I needed to make a decision, and the decision often had to do with men, as I was falling asleep I would say, "When I wake up, I want to know which way I am leaning."

When I am unsure of what I should do in my love life, and if my waking self isn't able to prompt my greater consciousness, I specifically ask for a dream to guide me. And I ask to be able to recall it. A remembered dream almost always comes when invited.

Don't defer your dreams! Once when I wanted dream guidance for finding a soul mate, I prepared my body to be as healthy and clear of energy blocks as possible. No wine, caffeine, sugared desserts or terrifying television news. Head on my lavender-laced pillow, suspending disbelief, I asked to be ready to receive. I expressed gratitude ahead of the gift I hoped for. The question as I drifted into sleep: "How will I find a man with whom I can connect more than I ever have before?"

When I awoke, I jotted down words and images from the dream. Wrote that I was kissing a stranger under an orange sky while my old love Peter, tiny, doll-like, looked on. I thought about what the dream meant to me. Why was Peter on my mind so many years later? I tuned into how I was feeling before I moved from the bed. I was sad. I was hopeful.

The next day, I noticed how external events began to align into synchronicity. Happy kissing couples zoomed into my attention. I saw a huge downtown billboard featuring an attractive couple with silver hair toasting each other with a cool brand of vodka. A friend told me that Peter had been in town, giving a lecture and, to my surprise, I felt almost no nostalgic nausea. My daughter gave me an orange fire opal (my birthstone) ring that she had made for me.

I anticipated that there would be help from others.

I didn't expect that my request would be answered in any particular way. I couldn't know then, that at a party that same evening, my daughter-in-law would be eyeing a charming acquaintance of my age group who had arrived without his girlfriend. "Wouldn't he be great for Elaine?" Melissa whispered to my son, Josh.

Months later, at another event, Josh asked the man if he were single. Double-take. "Not for me," my son joked. "I'd like you to meet my mom." "What about your dad?" asked David. "Oh, my mom likes to have flings once in a while." (Josh is a funny guy. I'd been divorced for eighteen years at that point.)

Remembering and writing down dream images can access our unconscious or half-conscious desires. A reflection triggered by those images provides a first step to manifesting our waking desires. We figure out what we really want by using the images, as we might use Tarot cards. We write from dreams to discover our hidden thought-forms.

Bring what you remember of your dream into focus and accept that you are receiving messages from the night country. Brainstorm (by clustering in your journal or with one of your friends or circles) how to eliminate obstacles. Choose to support your dream in as many ways as possible. Be ready to meet opportunities that you once might have dismissed. Don't worry about the future. And then, one day, in whatever form it comes, claim your dream.

I've dreamt in my life dreams that have stayed with me ever after, and changed my ideas; they've gone through and through me, like wine through water, and altered the colour of my mind.

Emily Bronte

Journal #10: *Pick one image from your dream and start writing. Keep going. How does your dream connect to what is going on in your life now?*

(October, 2006, dream) Live in a house with all women—nuns. Not allowed to sleep with men. Go to a club and see Peter who is doing a one-man comedy act. Peter comes back to sleep with me on the grey futon. So happy to be with him again for a night. The nuns help him to sneak upstairs.

Screen bulging near my bed. Squirrel trying to get in. I'm pushing against squirrel. Can feel squirmy fur against my hand. Keep it out. Thankful.

Kissing someone under an orange sky. A homunculus—Peter— looking on, says, "How can you go from one to another?"

I guess I still feel guilty about leaving Peter. He loved me and I loved him. But I couldn't believe in a future with him.

Journal #11: *Now ask, "What question do I have about the dream?"*

(October, 2006) Did I push Peter away because I couldn't commit? He promised that he would be faithful to me. People can change. Did I use my self-righteous morality as an excuse to flee from a love in which I had no control over my feelings? Am I a control freak or am I a wise woman to have not wanted a man who wanted other women?

Silver Fox Tip

To call for a dream, visualize walking down three steps—any steps, wood or cement, and then opening a door—any door, carved oak, aluminum screen, tacky door painted lucky red. This is an almost sure-fire way to invoke a dream. For remembering the dream, simply request that you will retain at least some of the dream. On awakening, remain still and tune into your feelings. Then record what you recollect.

-7-
Divination and Intuition

○ ○

Wherever you are...there you are. From *Alice in Wonderland*

Nora, the Celtic shaman, and I came upon two crow feathers in front of her cabin in the Vermont hills. "Let's call ourselves The Crow Sisters," she said as she picked them up and handed one to me. "How about if I guide you on a shamanic journey in exchange for a writing workshop? I won't go back to that class."

"Me neither," I agreed. "Although it's weirdly hypnotic watching that wrecking ball writer demolish each person's confidence."

"I was really looking forward to this writing week," said Nora. "Odd how all the others worship that sainted hypocrite."

After Nora brought out the screw-top red wine and two glasses borrowed from the dining hall, we sank into the Adirondack chairs on the deck of her cabin. She raised her glass and smiled, "Tell me, what would you like to happen next in your life?"

"Be able to really love a man," I answered.

"All your life you have been arguing and defending in order to connect with men," she said. "It's been a way of being loyal to your anxious ancestors. But your ancestors would be pleased to see you doing something different."

"Like what?"

46

"When you want to fight with a man, relax back into your spine and do Kegel exercises (slowly contracting and then relaxing the entire pelvic floor) at the same time. You'll find it hard to be trapped in knee-jerk rage when concentrating on these two movements."

I tried it. It works, although I often forget to relax and squeeze when I need it most.

◆　　　◆　　　◆

Shamanism

Shamanism is the world's oldest method of spiritual healing. The shaman does her work by entering deep states of consciousness in which awareness is expanded and information accessed. She acts as intermediary between what is known and what is unknown.

The shaman is a "wounded healer". She has navigated through a period of psychic crisis, through the shattering of an outward form of her life and the resulting chaos. Most single women over fifty could be amateur shamans, and we often play that kind of role with our friends without naming it as such. We understand each other because we all have been wounded. Most of us have gone through a time when everything in which we invested value began to be compromised, and we were left with only ourselves, without the labels that gave us identity. We had to let go of our attachment to a picture of ourselves that we had clung to like life boats in an unpredictable sea.

We can act as our own shamans when we write to retrieve information from previously hidden places. When we begin healing and living more authentically, we find that our most cherished assumptions about ourselves may not be true, and self-deception begins to disintegrate.

Nora also taught me the one-card layout, the easiest way to use the tarot. Tarot invites us to get more of what we want in life, and that includes our love lives. The cards provide a safe map for leaving the literal world for imaginative terrain.

Pick one card from a closed deck. Whichever card you choose is the perfect card. Ask what is going on in the card. Note everything you see. Then rewrite the basic elements—the actions and imagined feelings of the figures in the card, as if you were describing yourself in a story. What else do you see that is meaningful?

I selected a card from Nora's Transformational Tarot deck. The Queen of Cups, Water of Water. I admire water, its strength and resilience. It's non-adversarial flow. The positive aspects of water are associated with caring, compassion, receptivity. But my one detailed astrological chart shows that I am almost all air, a Libra, high-flying, with only a little earth for ballast, a little fire for manifestation. No water.

Nora interpreted, "In order to become the Queen of Cups, you have to surrender your overly strong will." She was dead on. I didn't know how to flow in a relationship. I was insensitive and combative with men when I felt powerless and unheard. My only option was to explain how bad and wrong they were in a high-pitched voice.

◆   ◆   ◆

I had decided at the age of five to be independent, charming, outgoing, and funny. I had decided never to cry. For most of my life I had no awareness of being lonely or depressed. I had often been told that I was "the most cheerful person" the teller had ever known.

What a joke that I picked an invitation to sit on a fluid throne. I have accrued losses: my once beloved husband, my mother, some cherished loves, the long time job which gave me meaning and community, my youth. Yet I couldn't cry until a time after I picked that card.

I was pushed onto a rudderless floating cup, forced to let go, to throw all my achievements and identities overboard in order to know the ocean, and perhaps myself. I can cry now, and partly because of that, have become more compassionate.

So here I am, an aging broad, without so many of the judgments that choreographed my life, the opinions that structured that life, the beliefs that framed it. Without the roles that once kept me fastened to my former way of being (mother, maverick teacher, wife), I'm not sure who I am or what I should do next. This water world is strange to me, but at least I'm sitting in a cup, weeping healing tears, with my turquoise-painted toes dangling in the sea air.

♦   ♦   ♦

Reiki

The practice of Reiki, working with vibrational energy, gave me another way to become both gentle and strong enough for egalitarian engagement with a man. By laying hands on oneself or another, or sending out intentional thought-forms, we transfer energy. Using Reiki, I can hold myself, mother myself, reach stillness, send intention, clear the clutter in my mind, listen carefully, and connect with others. Sometimes non-invasive touch is better than talk. I found the process valuable in relating to my mom when she was suffering from dementia.

With Reiki, I learned how to link up my imaginative mind with outside energy. I can send energy to my past or my future for healing (using an old photo for the past). Anyone can do this with faith and imagination. You don't have to have Reiki training, although it's an advantage.

And, hey, you can Reiki the guy before you meet him! Just clear your mind, and send an intention out for the best possible outcome of the first meeting.

Ask for help from whomever and whatever you believe in—angels, guides, teachers. Ask for help with the aid of divination devices. To "divine" means "to know the will of the gods." Divination devices (I Ching, Tea Leaves, Runes, Tarot Cards, The Pendulum, Angel Cards) can transport you along the psychic pathway. Reiki, Shamanic rituals, dance, yoga, free painting, and meditation are other methods of moving toward deep recognition. Writing immediately after using any of these can take you further into awareness. As well, automatic writing (the writing that seems to be coming from a supernatural pipeline, not just from within you), can get you in touch with your not-easily-accessed knowing. All these strategies can channel your unacknowledged knowledge and develop your intuition.

◆   ◆   ◆

Intuition

Intuition is the ability to read a person or situation without the step-by-step process of logic. An intuitive person can pick up many clues instantly, and "know" what to do or say without necessarily being able to explain why. The answers are within you.

Intuition is a way of bringing us into a direct experience of the real. It is a skill based on attentiveness. Maintaining mindfulness, the minute-to-minute awareness of what is, helps cut through confusion. It's important to pay attention to our instincts when we are unsure about whether to write back to a guy on the internet, go out on a first date with a new admirer, tell our truth to a man, or whether or not to leave him.

If only I had paid attention to my gut when I first met Michael at a Portuguese bakery. By the time I had eaten three custard tarts, I had fallen for that Spencer Tracy look-alike. He punctuated his attentive listening with dry wit, and I felt overly disappointed when he suddenly jumped up, paid the bill, muttered something apologetic, and ran. I was so happy when he called the next day to ask me out that I ignored my muddled and squashed recognition that a man who behaves like a frightened gerbil is not a man ready for a real relationship.

Intuition gives that first flash of knowledge, although reason can make valuable revisions to a response or decision. But you have to trust yourself before you can trust your inner voice. Before you know and accept yourself as fully as possible, that voice may well be unreliable. It may be a cry from your greedy or baby self demanding—right now!—whatever attracts you.

Once you have learned to trust yourself, it's your heart that leads in matters of the heart. If you follow your intuition, using your logical mind as a second opinion, you can have faith that you are making the best decision possible.

If your head rules your heart, you might make an apparently sound decision that doesn't bring you happiness. You might decide that a decent reliable guy is a good bet, even though he doesn't turn you on and you don't feel the kind of connection with him that you dream of with a lover. If you allowed yourself to tune into your emotional body, you might feel a depletion of energy, an indication of the incompleteness of rationality.

I left a decent man, the protection of position and money, and the comfort of a known world for both me and my children. My inner voice insisted that I must go, and so I left. The price has been high. I hurt people I cared about. I dropped through a loophole in good society. **Splat!** Now I am just another aging single woman, a former schoolteacher living in an apartment on a half pension, not sure about very much. But I awake each morning with zest for the day.

Even when we have become psychically strong, intuition can be blocked. Sometimes other people can sabotage your energy flow with their clogged energy, or anger, or pressuring need. Sometimes we block ourselves. Some self-blocks to intuition are: living at a frantic pace, chosen numbness (wine, sweets, romantic fiction), unfocused attention, disorganization, resentments, and simply not believing in intuition as a valuable tool.

Choose one of your blocks, and perform a ritual by putting on paper words such as: "I now let go of my resentment of …my ex-husband, my last lover, the woman who took away my first lover..." (earth); read it aloud, perhaps to one of your circles (air); burn it in a safe place, such as your kitchen sink (fire); then put out the fire by turning on the tap (water).

To help develop your intuitive muscle you could: 1) use divination devices; 2) focus your intent and pay attention; 3) spend time in nature, preferably in solitude; 4) practice some form of meditation; 5) tell your truth (to yourself and others); 6) keep an open heart and an open mind; 7) take a course on awakening intuition; 8) reinforce this practice by keeping a journal.

Try the "I am psychic" game. Take a few deep breaths, and, for example, guess which elevator is coming of the three, or guess who is calling you when the phone rings. It doesn't matter if you get it wrong. It's good practice for insight training.

To increase your sense of knowing whether a man could be good for you, ask your inner voice for guidance. Slow down, ground yourself, notice what you feel, notice what he says and does, write your impressions in your journal, and ask for signs. Signs that have meaning for you will be visible on book covers, ads on streetcars, spray-painted graffiti, or a scene you see on the street. You may be driving and hear an old song on the car radio that resonates. I once heard Leonard Cohen's "Bird on a Wire" in such a situation, although I wasn't entirely sure which of us was the bird.

Think of intuition as a pair of magic glasses to wear while dating. Tra-la!   You will *know* what is right to do even if you would rather, for example, fall for a sexy charming but unreachable man. Attuned to insight, you can see through the fake, deceptive, or deceitful protective covering of a wrong-for-you wooer.

The only really valuable thing is intuition. Albert Einstein

Journal #12: *Think of a problem. Using one of your psychic tools—pendulum, tarot cards, rune stones etc.—to guide you, ask a specific question. Answer by writing for ten minutes. Don't think. Observe what surfaces.*

Journal #13: *Take a small shamanic trip. Close your eyes and let your imagination lead you to a land where you meet a spirit guide (perhaps an animal totem will appear) and he/she/it helps you do what you need to do.*

(Spring, 1990)
Walking a yellow brick road
paved with gold paved with self-help books
I step on a crack and break my mother and
meet a wizard who can't help me
but he's cute and I still want him.
He leads me to a stage set—says—
"Don't think, don't read so much"
and I don't know how to exit
so the audience still loves me
or how to break the spell
when a doe bursts through the backdrop
puts my palm against my green heart
and I rise above the construct
of an unloved house with pillars
lifted by the light
in her warm brown eyes that know me

Silver Fox Tip

To develop your intuitive powers, ask yourself "What if I knew?" when you feel uncertain or doubtful, and then see what appears.

-8-
Deep Listening

○ ○

Almost all of our sadnesses are moments of paralysis of feeling when we can no longer hear our surprised feelings living.

Rainer Maria Rilke

A Silver Fox listens carefully to others and to the world. She hears the societal aversion to aging women, and resists it. This foxy lady has shed any internalized repugnance to her aging body, and sends out sexy vixen vibes.

Other women will take notice and be inspired. Men will hear her siren song and be enchanted.

As well, a Silver Fox listens to her own wants and needs. A different kind of listening is necessary if we are to attend to ourselves as we never have before. Deep listening reveals the real and is a path to intimacy—intimacy first with ourselves. When we write down the surprising words we hear, they are preserved on a page, last summer's juicy peaches, to be reread in winter, letting us know and understand ourselves. A journal can be a hearing aid, if we activate it with our attention. With concentration, time and solitude, unexpected perceptions emerge and bloom. Your real voice calls from the page.

When you listen to yourself through writing, you might start to think about when and why you stopped making decisions based on what is good for you. You can note which of your words and phrases have a magic glitter for you. You can observe which dramas you indulge in. You can notice the people, objects or places that jump-start your senses into aliveness. Insights encoded on the page become illuminated.

Once you become a better listener, you will listen more acutely to men, giving yourself the gift of self-preservation. You will be able to hear in your gut, in your bones, what you would rather not know about someone to whom you are madly attracted. When your instincts go against your wants, when you can't deny or rationalize because you really heard him, you might save yourself heartbreak, or worse—wasted years, the crash of self-esteem, a depleted bank account—by accepting simple disappointment.

Often we don't want to hear that it is better for us to give up our pleasures and addictions. You have to allow yourself to hear that you should not enter a relationship with a certain delicious man, or that you must leave a lover you delight in. It was only by rereading seven of my journals that I was able to accept that Peter would never be a good mate for me.

Simone Weil, a French philosopher, said that there was only one thing worth asking another person when you meet him, whether an old friend or a new acquaintance: "What are you dealing with right now in your life?" If you are exchanging your answers to that question with another, perhaps a man you are learning to love, listen for a different set of possibilities. Allow yourself to recognize and perhaps set aside your prejudices. I used to shut off when a man revealed his unacceptable—to me—politics. I didn't give him a chance, although he might have been a much better man to a woman than the charming, angry lefties I've often fallen for.

If you listen attentively, without your biases acting as filters, to what a man tells you about himself, he is more likely reveal his otherness, his way of being, different from your assumptions. You will be able to hear what he is actually saying, what he means, who he is.

That kind of listening heals the suffering of not being heard. Most of us, men and women, have been deprived of non-judgmental attention. Offering others the gift of being understood is one of the ways of loving well and creating communion. Listening well is part of the key to your becoming irresistible.

In the course of a day, listen as much as you can in a conscious way. Listen with your "inner ear" for subtext in conversation, beauty in a shrieking siren, ugliness in too-sweet compliments. Yet it is also sensible to practice discrimination, protecting yourself from what you would rather not listen to. I often close my ears to the following: 1) gossip when it feels like a mud bath; 2) repetitious whining; 3) bullying radio talk shows except for the one my son co-hosts; 4) the heavy footsteps of my charming upstairs neighbour.

I can be a dominating talker, and can enslave others by my need to talk. Having experienced entrapment when someone imposed that need on me, I am trying in conversation to be aware of when I monopolize a conversation. When another person is talking to me, I struggle to neither give advice, nor shove in my own similar experiences. I try not to analyze or interpret the teller's story. I make an effort to give my whole attention to the other. I listen as I could never listen when I was young and tone deaf.

I also notice the way I am listened to. As Anton and I were driving home from a Mindfulness Meditation weekend, I was revealing something intense about my life when he started singing. In response to my furious reaction, he said he could listen and sing at the same time.

When I narrow my attention to relate to a piece of art, sometimes asking it what it wants to tell me, I feel happy. In a jazz cafe, there is a particular pleasure in tracking only the bittersweet voice of a saxophone in a trio. Out in nature, I might ask a tree or a rose for advice. If I listen to the wind's reminder that I am here *right now*, I am sharply conscious of the luck of being alive.

A wonderful way to listen to and hear your own mind has been created by Linda Trichter Metcalf and Tobin Simon (www. pwriting.org) for their **Proprioceptive Method,** a slow and thoughtful approach to journaling which engenders self-trust. The method facilitates our checking in with our unidentified thoughts as means to a more authentic life. (*Proprioceptive* describes the body's sense of itself. Metcalf and Simon use the term metaphorically, comparing the mind's capacity to know itself to the body's knowing, for example, how to pick up a glass of water.)

The technique consists of twenty-five minute sessions of writing while listening to Baroque music. Each session is called a **Write**, and is guided by three simple rules and self-directed. The Write is always "perfect" even if you are critical about the feelings expressed. The glow of a candle illuminating the ritual separates a special time and space from ordinary life.

Imagine giving voice to your thoughts as you think them. Pretend to be speaking on paper. When you read over your writing, listen to yourself, and trust what you hear. You are building awareness and self-confidence. You are awakening what Metcalf and Simon call the *auditory imagination*—the capacity to enter your thoughts in an interested, nonjudgmental way and gain awareness of yourself from them. You begin to imagine your thoughts as a persona with a voice.

♦   ♦   ♦

The three rules are:

1) Imagine your thoughts as spoken words and write them exactly as if you could hear them, as they occur to you moment by moment.

2) Listen to what you write—the "listening presence" never judges, edits, or censors.

3) Be ready to ask the proprioceptive question: "What do I mean by _____?"

As you move along, continue to ask yourself what you mean by a word or phrase you've written. This allows you to explore your thoughts and enter them more deeply.

Resist the temptation to revise your **Write** while reading it through. As Metcalf and Simon say, "You're not responsible for your thoughts—you didn't choose them." If you feel uncomfortable (or wonderful), you can deal with those feelings when addressing the four concluding questions.

1) What thoughts were heard but not written? What did I think and not write?
2) How or what do I feel now?
3) What larger story is this **Write** a part of? Consider the larger personal meaning of your written thoughts.
4) What ideas came up for future **Writes**?

If we had a keen vision and feeling of all ordinary human life, it would be like hearing the grass grow and the squirrel's heart beat, and we should die of that roar which lies on the other side of silence. George Eliot, Middlemarch

Journal #14: *A* **Write** : *What Are My Heart's Desires? Keep asking the proprioceptive question, "What do I mean by...?"*

(Spring, 2007) Most of all, I want to love and be loved. What do I mean by love? Feeling at home with someone, safe, energized, having fun, laughing, working, playing, planning together. Trust. That will take time. What do I mean by "take time?" Whatever time it takes to meet someone, and time to trust that the other means well, and more, to trust that I won't react in my old way, at least not too often. What do I mean by "my old way"? Fearful, angry, my freedom or self image seemingly on the line, and then attacking, bitching, venting, making assumptions.

What are my other desires? More deep connection with work and place. What do I mean by connection? The joy of union, of being my true self and at the same time being able to forget myself.

Journal #16: *A time of being heard, a time of not being heard, a time of my not listening well*

A Time when I was Heard (Barbara is my younger and only sister)

(November 23, 1993) Dear Barbara, You have listened to me. Once again I say to you, without you I would have had no understanding of intimacy when I was growing up. You saved my life, not my physical life, but the spark I have been able to bellow in the past years to create a life so joyful that I can't believe I am living *this* way, rather than *that* way. A slight shift (after years of preparation) and I find myself hiking up this higher mountain , with the light clearer, the air thinner, the way cleaner.

I love you, and am every day grateful for your existence. E.

A Time When I Was Not Heard (from "Mother")

What have you got to be depressed about?
You have a good mother and father
A nice home
Friends
You're good at school, clever, pretty, young, only 16
Why are you talking about depression?
If only I'd had what you have
I would have given anything
to have what you have
You're the luckiest little girl in the world.

(A time when I didn't listen well)

(April 24, 1996, 4:12 AM) Woke up feeling horrible. Remembering last night on the phone with Anton, when he told me about the morale at his office. I responded with what I'm starting to see as my self-absorption, my inability to really listen to another person, anothers' problems. I boasted about my temperament, about being able to still enjoy the moment even though I have many problems. I was like my father at his worst.

Silver Fox Tip

For one time, listen to the man in your life, or the man-to-come-next, without any judgment, creating room for him to be completely open (you can be critical later).

The spirit is the conscious ear. Emily Dickinson

-9-
Personal Power

○ ○

A woman must have money and a room of her own...

Virginia Woolf

A room of one's own isn't nearly enough. A house, or, best an island of one's own. Lillian Hellman

Women often give away power. Most of us were trained to do so through subtle control methods, by guilt, judgment, or patterns of obligation. Often it was done "for our own good" – to prepare us to "fit in", and to win a male. If our willfulness were not bound, so the thinking went, we might become failures at work, with friends, and in the marriage market.

For years I put others' needs first. I didn't want anyone to be angry at me. I believed I had to see all the people in my life at regular intervals in order to deposit my assurance that they were liked. I would put aside my writing schedule, or my wish for time alone. I was on a merry-go-round of coffees and lunches and dinners with friends and acquaintances.

Free-floating guilt causes us to be too good for our own good. I'm a recovering people pleaser but I still give away time when I don't want to, still work at being good company, and often continue to say "yes" to whatever is being asked. (My mother's oft-repeated best compliment about another woman was that "she would do anything for anyone.") Sometimes I don't say my truth, and at other times I worry that I've been offensive in saying my truth.

The big mistake in being too compliant often comes from undervaluing oneself. Many women have revealed how they were endlessly nice and infinitely forgiving to guys who couldn't be there for them. They felt sorry for those men who were so busy at work, so tired, and, poor things, so scared of intimacy.

I can't remember where I read the following sentence, but I love it. Nice is just another word for victim.

Our obligatory niceness often makes it harder for us to speak up in personal situations. Here are some lines that I should have said. What are yours?

1) Just because you need me doesn't mean that's how I choose to spend my time.
2) Don't patronize me, kid, I gave you life.
3) You bore me.
4) I don't want to go out with you again because you in-terrupted my every sentence.
5) You can give me unsolicited advice once you live your own life perfectly.
6) You may be a moral Marxist, but I know what you've done.
7) I don't want to, no, I won't. NO!

When we give away our power, we suffer from depen-dence on others for our self-definition. We show evidence of boundary problems, distractibility, and underdevelopment of the self.

I still sometimes lose power by swallowing tiny tyrannies while smiling. I've demoralized myself by retelling painful childhood events, second-guessing someone's "real" motiva-tion towards me, compromising and deferring and then feeling lousy and resentful. I can regress into the old self-defeating habit of downplaying my strengths.

It's so easy for me to let a man do all the driving (and not just the car), to twist myself to accommodate to his needs and schedule, to spend time with him when I'd rather have time for myself. I have to resist my conditioning.

Now, much of the time, I find I can choose to please myself because I am too old (yes, in a good way) to reduce myself, or to fit into someone else's agenda. I speak up when I'm uncomfortable. I'm more careful of how I spend my time and give myself time to think before I rush to being helpful. Today my test of whether a choice is right for me is if I feel happy and at peace with it.

Self-nurturing helps. One way to nurture yourself is to tame your inner critic. Usually the internalized voice of a critical parent or teacher regaling you with *their s*tuff, the internal critic can sometimes give good advice. By making friends with her, you are in a better position to train her to help you. The judgmental mind responds best to kindness and understanding. Start by drawing her, giving her a name (mine is Nastalya), and asking her what she wants from you. Listen to her counsel. Another technique for self-support is "self-talk" (allaying anxiety by talking yourself through it). A third method is to recall difficult periods which you survived. You have lived to tell the tale of, for example, how you were picked on when you were growing up, the teacher who told you that you would never amount to anything, or the guys who didn't like you as much as you liked them. Have you endured a divorce or a serious illness? Can you now appreciate any positives that came from those negative situations?

I think that the best mind-set for attracting a man who treats you well is: "Life is good—I'd prefer to have a lover, but it can be whenever, whatever..." We should emulate those teenagers who wear T-shirts with **WHATEVER** inscribed on the chest, a word representing the attitude they adopt for meeting our worries about them. Imagine wearing that T-shirt while dating.

Men sense our independence and self-esteem. They can also pick up any whiff of desperation, no matter how vivacious and perky we present. What we really have to offer is who we actually are, and we can't help sending out vibrations that others pick up.

I believe in honesty, and think "The Rules" (the rules for catching a man by playing hard-to-get) are ridiculous and tiring. But really accepting that you don't have to do all the work, all the compromising, all the chasing, and all the swallowing of your own preferences, can only be a good thing when you enter into a relationship. That can only happen if you believe that you're worth being courted. (Yes, you can court too. Why not if you fancy the guy? But do it from a position of strength.)

Once you know yourself pretty well, you will know what kind of man you want. And when you meet him, you will have the confidence to ask what he wants from a relationship. Just about every man will tell you the truth. Could save you years!

The law of attraction is a cliché but I think it's real. We've all been working this law somewhat unconsciously, and the more we become conscious, the more we can create the reality that is the best for us. The intention to increase personal power sets in motion forces that bring to us the right teacher, the right book, the right friend, the right challenge that we are ready to meet, and perhaps the right man. We often receive what we ask for, although not necessarily in an anticipated form or a time frame.

When we lose focus, we lose energy. We don't have to rush to regain that energy, just hang with our low energy until we find a remedy. Meditation, therapy and companionable books have ameliorated my chronic anxiety. One or more of the following are useful in returning me to my strong self: Nia dance, yoga, biking, daily journal writing, talking to friends and family, flirting, white wine (Chablis when I can afford it), love, Belgian chocolate, reading and writing fiction, my children's company, bouncing on my little trampoline while belting out sixties folk songs (Phil Ochs at the moment), music (Mozart always works), hiking in the woods or on mountains, teaching—and I could go on!

Emotions can't be controlled—it's their nature to be unstable. Don't judge yourself if you feel many things during a day. You're not hysterical, not out of control, not crazy if you are able to feel a wide band of emotions. If you can pause and not act them out (most of the time), you're healthy and less tamped down than many in our society.

Can you acknowledge when you have acted out of a wish to punish, withdraw from, or batter your lover? The more I get to know my own fallibilities and my dark shadow side, the more I have the power to understand and forgive myself (and him!) for being not-perfect. We all sometimes regress when we're hurt or angry, no matter how much work we've done, but owning and self-regulating our emotions and taking responsibility for our unkind actions limits damage and makes it easier for another to forgive us.

Work is another way to feel our power in the world, our "power with" rather than "power over", as we second wave feminists used to say. You could remind yourself of all your accomplishments by writing your work *curriculum vitae,* starting from your first lemonade stand or the play you wrote in Grade 2. Make a list of what you are most proud of in your work life to remind you of your competence and triumphs.

Even if you are content in your work life, but especially if you are not satisfied, visualize alternate work lives, perhaps as preparation for a different job or career after you "retire".

Back when I was teaching full time, I happened into a tearoom. Mary, the owner, was in her 70s and read tea leaves. She had chartreuse hair, and wore army boots, a recycled tie-dyed T-shirt, and a fringed suede jacket from Kensington Market's second-hand street. She told me her story.

Mary had been a math teacher in Toronto for twenty-one years. One day, after drinking a cup of Earl Grey in the staffroom, she thought the leaves from the split tea bag formed a path leading to place she believed she was meant to visit. She got up, and walked out of the school, wearing—she remembered—black patent pumps, a pencil skirt and a blouse that tied at the neck with a bow. Never looked back. Got sick leave for stress. Went to Guatemala, worked at a restaurant on Lake Atitlan, became an artist and a psychic, and took a much younger lover.

When she looked at my leaves, she saw a similar path. I left the tearoom, and then left a safe teaching position at a school where my students were bright, generous-spirited and fun, and my colleagues were dear respected friends. But teaching there had become too easy in a certain way. I wanted new learning curves and I wanted mountains. I took a job in Switzerland.

We women have not taken up our fair share of space in the world, although as we age, many of us are breaking out of the straightjacket of constraint. Personal physical space is one means to psychic space. My bedroom has trippy teal walls, an ochre duvet cover, and secrets in the pillows encased in a (tasteful) wild animal and naked man print. The art promises transformation, from the butterfly emerging into a goddess to the pottery portrait of lovebirds in flight. Strands of sadness are woven into the ruby and gold Oaxacan rugs on either side of the bed. My bedroom signals that I don't have to be good, not in the old way—just have to give what I can give—me.

We have been taught to keep ourselves small. When I was growing up in the fifties in Toronto, there was only one way for a nice girl to sit in a chair, and it wasn't with her legs apart. I was taught not to talk too much (it didn't take), not to win at games (always forgot), not even to put up my hand in class to answer questions (intimidating to boys). But we didn't diet—my friends and I ate a cheesecake at least once a week all through high school. Yet now, even though I am resistant to the culture of anorexia (to the extent of eating three desserts a day), I am influenced by the incredible pressure for women to keep themselves small. I think about my weight way too much.

Just to give ourselves more room, more self-confidence, maybe we should think about saying whatever we want as long as it's kind (for example, discussing menopause at dinner parties), wearing outsize dramatic hats while journaling, strutting as if we were goddesses, and having the audacity to call attention to our fabulous selves by wearing clothes we once avoided as too sexy or bold. Do we dare display a home-made bumper sticker that boasts: OLD, FOXY, AND PROUD!

I am my own heroine.

Marie Bashkirtseff
(19th century musician, occultist)

Journal #17: How were you able to say your (uncomfortable) truth to someone close to you? What gave you the courage to speak?

(December, 1992) I told my father (who was dying and in pain) that I didn't like it that he had diminished me at times when I was young. I was determined to get as clear with him as I could before he died, and he came through in a wonderful way. He listened carefully to me, and then acknowledged that he had put me down and was sorry. Also, he told me how much he thought of me and admired me.

If we can't tell the truth about ourselves, how can we tell the truth about others? Virginia Woolf

Journal #18: *Write your own eulogy. Praise yourself for the life you are living, for the life you intend to live.*

(February, 1992) Elaine was so extraordinarily filled with life that it's hard to believe that she's dead. She always had an idea on the go, laughed a lot, loved to be with people, do things, go places, and share what she had with her friends and family. She was fun and generous and caring. She was a good mother who was able to break some of the patterns from her own childhood and to really come through for her children.

Elaine was very brave and dared to do what she needed to do in spite of her many fears. She became a role model by her bravery, her sharing, her insistence on a fair life for herself and others, and her vitality. She was creative and enriched others' lives with her creativity.

She will be missed. Often someone will think, "If only I could talk to Elaine."

Journal #19: *Here's to your name! An over-the-top speech by Sherry Champagne, the celebrating goddess.*

(Journal, September 2007) Here's to Elaine. Drink a glass. Drink a bottle! Don't hold back. We're all here to celebrate that exciting, entrancing, exuberant, excellent, ebullient Elaine. Thousands of you have gathered in this crowded bar to raise a glass to the eternal, if not easy, Elaine. She's charming, ageless, fun, and sexy. Those of you who think a woman can't be hot over sixty have revised that myth by looking at our Elaine. All together now, ELAINE!!

Silver Fox Tip

*Accept that you're going to die. That acceptance gives you power, and steadies you into spending your time and energy wisely. (**Fugit hora, memento mori!** Time flies, remember you must die!)*

Between two evils, I always pick the one I never tried before.

Mae West

-10-
Affordable Luxury

○ ○

I have the greatest of all riches: that of not desiring them.

Isadora Duncan

A Silver Fox looks after her money. The prince has gone, or at any rate revealed his frogginess. Her youth has gone. Some opportunities have disappeared. She knows how important it is to create a secure future, while enjoying the present.

Money buys independence in love. There is enormous freedom in needing a lover only for love. As well, money buys the pleasure that help us look and feel good: those hand-milled soaps, natural face creams, unassuming little wines, theatre performances, and travel to far-off places. Money allows us to be generous, both with others and ourselves. To have personal power, it's essential to have enough money.

What amount is enough? Remarkably little, if you're resourceful and your priority is living the life you want over accumulating all the things we are supposed to want. You have options.

Continuing to make money is often a necessity. Many divorcing women don't ask for alimony—I didn't. Some of us have lost money on the stock market. Many don't have a pension, don't own property, and don't have much equity. And we're going to be living longer.

But making money can also be a pleasure. A lot of us were out of the workplace during the years of raising children and then found the excitement of entering into the wider world, to relish competence and experience the excitement of being a player.

There are a variety of ways to make money. Some women have given up the pleasures in the abundant free time of retirement to take full-time positions, often in NGOs or government. A former professor (whom I like for many reasons, including her fixing me up with several eligible men) now sits on appeal hearings for the Workplace Safety and Insurance Board of Ontario.

I know women enjoying jobs that they would have turned their younger noses up at, and loving those jobs. Friends and acquaintances are finding satisfaction in, for example, managing a gallery, working in a bookstore, selling Murano glass items in a charming boutique, bartending, landscape gardening—the list goes on. A burnt-out teacher I know is now a cleaning lady and relishes her autonomy and the novel experience of being appreciated and sought after.

I know sixty-something women who are new entrepreneurs. Some have started consulting businesses, selling the expertise they gained in various jobs and careers. The spectrum goes from advising government ministries to private tutoring. Others are marketing skills they wouldn't have thought of exchanging for money earlier in their lives: catering, baking brilliant cookies, sewing quilts, landscape gardening, personal organizing. One acquaintance created remunerative work aligned with her ethical beliefs. She has a direct trading relationship with two women's groups in Bolivia, and runs a small business importing their handicrafts.

My small business, "Pen & Purpose", includes editing, teaching courses as a freelance journaling coach, and producing workshops.

Many women have trouble asking for enough money for their work. I have been one of them, and am learning not to feel unworthy of receiving. If we don't ask for what we are worth, we are undermining ourselves. Volunteering to give time and expertise is a different matter, as is charging a sliding scale as an act of social consciousness.

If you need to be careful with your money, and you don't want paying work, you could cut back and down. Buy at yard sales and off Craig's List, delight in a tent instead of a hotel room, turn down the heat in your place. You could ditch your cell phone (how many times do you have a phone-necessary crisis, and what are the odds that if you ask for help, he will be an axe murderer?). Get rid of cable. Use the public library, for movies and music as well as books. Go to museums at free times, look for complimentary tickets to plays or go to pay-what-you can shows, attend gallery openings, bookstore readings, and free concerts.

I know women who have never bought property, and who rent modest flats in safe unflashy neighbourhoods. Some of them, and others with houses or condos, only buy clothing at secondhand shops. There are contented women who never get expensive haircuts. Some never travel unless they're camping or visiting friends or relatives. Dining out is a rare occasion for many, and friends exchange dinner party invitations instead of meeting at a restaurant. Cooking and eating locally grown produce can lead to healthier eating, delicious meals, good cheer, and way less expense.

Some women make all their presents, giving their time and creativity and skill. One friend initiated a Christmas and birthday present idea: you can only give something you own, something that is good but no longer "yours", in the sense of your feeling aligned to who you are now.

Working vacations are another way to go. Women of a certain age have enjoyed being *Willing Workers on Organic*

Farms, doing *Habitat for Humanity* work, and participating in other volunteer vacations. There are books and websites giving information on those kinds of holidays.

I chopped vegetables in exchange for what would have been a thousand dollar yoga vacation at Kripalu, a spiritual community in Massachusetts; taught journaling at an arts school in northern British Columbia in exchange for airfare and a private cabin under a mountain and beside a spring; stripped paint from window frames for a brush painting workshop at a Zen monastery and a further stab at enlightenment—all when I was over fifty. Most of my peers were college students who adopted me as a cute older mascot. If I had paid for those holidays, I would have missed out on the engagement from being a semi-insider, friendships, and the learning that came from being outside my age-appropriate box.

If you have some money, you can gather air miles in various ways. I have a Visa card that I use for everything, including groceries, in order to accrue points. Most of my air travel is to visit friends or relatives, or to fly to affordable countries. Exchanging residences is another great way to see the world, and the opportunity to become much more than a tourist. I'm on a senior's home exchange site for a one-time $100 cost. So far, I have done two exchanges, one with a woman in Paris, and another with a couple who live on the gorgeous Sunshine Coast of British Columbia. Both times I was invited over by neighbours, and got to know local shopkeepers. You don't need to own your place to do an exchange.

A road trip, such as one I took with my daughter, can include staying at sanctuaries. We spent time at the Kushi Institute (the centre for macrobiotic cooking in Massachusetts) on a work holiday. For little cost, we slept in dorms at convents and monasteries. At one Buddhist monastery in West Virginia, we did work exchange in return for a room and wonderful vegetarian Thai meals. My daughter chopped wood; I shelled peas and gave a donation for the inspiring teaching. We made friends there with whom we stayed at their centuries-old home near a Appalachian trailhead, and we also visited old friends along the way. As well, we enjoyed stays with *Servas* volunteers (a wonderful peace organization that promotes hospitality to participants from other countries).

Having a large life does not depend on a large income.

Money is of value for what it buys, and in love it buys time, place, intimacy, comfort, and a private corner alone.

Mae West

Journal #20: *What is your relationship with money? Describe feelings of shame, greed, generosity, distortion, comfort and discomfort.*

(Winter, 2002) I've had trouble asking clients for the money my time and expertise is worth. I've felt compelled to split a restaurant bill even if the cost was wildly unequal. I've hesitated to remind someone that he or she owed me money. I used to think those feelings came from my being such a generous person. Well, I am generous, but, after a certain point, I become measuring and resentful. Luckily, age and good advice are helping me get over my fear of being real instead of overgenerous.

Once upon a very long time ago, I wasn't concerned about money. My parents, though far from rich, made sure my sister and I didn't have to worry. I didn't register that living above my father's tailoring store could mean that I was worth less than my friends in upper middle class homes (one in a mansion), and, as far as I know, no one else did until I dated a wealthy boy in my late teens. In my semi-nomadic twenties, I wasn't bothered about money. When I was married I didn't have to think about it. Later, I kept earning enough to live well on a fairly small amount. Now, with a tiny pension (and grateful for it although ruing my ignorance in cashing it in twice when I was younger and wanted to travel, and then not contributing to it when I had the chance), and with advancing age, I think about money more than I ever have. But I still don't worry a lot.

Silver Fox Tip

If you are not sure you want to buy something, whether it is a jacket or a fancy condiment or a stock, wait at least a day until you are clear.

Happiness consists not in having much, but in being content with little. Countess of Blessington

-11-
New Aging

○ ○

Age doesn't protect you from love, but love, to some extent, protects you from age. Jeanne Moreau

A Silver Fox doesn't live in an age ghetto. When she meets someone, she asks herself, "Do we connect soul to soul? Will this teenager be my friend? Could this man in his eighties, or thirties, be my lover?"

She refuses to internalize the judgment of others who might be saying "It's so pathetic to want this or that other thing, or especially *this,* at your age". She resists letting the outside world define her and rejects unnecessary societal limits attempting to keep the fox in her place. She's never too old or set in her ways to try something new (other than, perhaps, becoming a prima ballerina or beginning a career as a Hollywood ingénue).

She experiences all her emotions but does not indulge in negativity. The glass, even if chipped and cracked, can still be half full. A sense of humour helps.

She supports other women. For her, taking care of other women is like taking care of herself. If she's a social activist, one of her causes is helping her aging sisters.

She connects strongly with the girl she was before she turned ten, the girl who wasn't afraid to speak up, and wasn't worried about boys liking her, or girls freezing her out, or teachers being angry if she didn't behave. After the age of ten, she was encouraged to become a Pleaser, discouraged from being her spirited self.

During puberty, I, along with most of my peer group, got co-opted into being "nice". Before, I was a girl who dared to climb bridges seventy feet above the ground, a girl who wasn't afraid of parents, teachers, cops, or other kids. I splashed water on my face to hide tears whenever my mother yelled at lunch time, and then went back to school, and had a great time. I was competitive in the classroom. I played "teacher" with other kids as students, wrote novels, directed plays, and was chosen to be the school representative on special occasions. As the first of my friends to get my period, at the age of eleven, I liked dispensing wisdom and advice.

Although others looking on might not agree, I feel I have been lucky in my life, and especially lucky that the young girl who was so intrepid and alive never got completely squashed. Today I have given up *nice*. In Latin, *nice* means ignorant, not knowing. In Old English, *nice* means foolish, and, in Old French, stupid and foolish.

A Silver Fox takes care of her health, eats locally grown food when possible, resists unnecessary medical intervention, and chooses a pro-active and positive attitude. She doesn't let her body become prematurely old. I've found body work helpful in undoing the ways my body had become constricted. It took years of yoga (mellow Iyengar), Feldenkrais work, the Alexander technique, deep tissue massage, and the personal set of meditative stretching exercises I do daily to straighten my slightly humped back and sloping shoulders. Nowadays I also dance several times a week, walk, hike, cycle, and bounce on my mini-trampoline. I think it's important to do some exercise, but only in ways that you really enjoy.

I also treat myself to good face creams, and not the ones that sell for hundreds of dollars in fancy department stores. I use a wild-crafted-plants cream made by an herbalist friend, feeding my appreciative skin and nurturing a micro-economy.

A Silver Fox looks after her money—sex, love, relationships are important, but money matters too. As I suggested in Chapter 10, it's crucial to be wise about money. Most of us are going to be living longer than our mothers, without the financial security of a marriage which few of them left, no matter how unhappy they were. There's a big money gap between single men and women over fifty. Women not only have less money than men, but countless women live below the poverty line. Among other challenges, it's hard to enter the dating world if we are not financially self-sufficient. To a large extent, our happiness with a man depends on not needing him for his money.

Yet in a more favourable way, women and men become more alike as we age. Both genders often develop parts of ourselves that have lain undeveloped. Many women start involving themselves in challenging volunteer or paid work, and a lot of men begin slowing down, becoming more sensitive and nurturing. In later life men and women can find a lot of common ground. We can understand each other more than before, learn from each other, and support each other through the challenges of aging.

Beginning a love affair in our later years can be an exhilarating experience. As we age, we come to think differently about ourselves and see that we're acting differently. We know ourselves better and act on what we know. We have shed many ill-fitting conventions in order to be true to ourselves. Self-trust has increased each time we have acted courageously and in tune with who we are. We have learned to protect ourselves from things we simply don't wish to do. We can love happily because we are more real, more autonomous, more willing to express our real feelings, more able to accept ourselves and others as we actually are, without fantasy, denial, or image management. We get it that we will never be completely "together", that all of us are scarred. We can be vulnerable and strong, having given up trying to live up to what we think we should be.

I have taken a vow that I will not settle for less than what I truly desire. So there are rules that I must break. There are situations and people I must say *no* to.

Things I've said no to: having a dog at this point in my life, taking care of needy men, eating more than I really want to in order to make someone else happy. I have almost stopped my habit of "helpful" interfering. I have been letting go of people who drain me.

On the other hand, I think we should say *yes* to things which we usually refuse. If we hide our frailties and destructive sides, if we are afraid to leap out of our ruts and go after what we truly desire, we are in effect suppressing our sexual essence. We are holding ourselves back from real living. While we have juice in us, let's just say *yes!* Remember the famous passage in *Ulysses* in which Molly cries, "…he could feel my breasts all perfume yes and his heart was going like mad and yes I said yes I will Yes."

When opportunity knocks, just say yes!

Age puzzles me. I thought it was a quiet time. My seventies were interesting, and fairly serene, but my eighties are passionate. I grow more intense as I age. Florida Scott-Maxwell

Journal #21: Write a letter to a grandchild, real or imaginary, telling what it's like to be 80.

(To my imaginary granddaughter) Sweetie, it's amazing to be 80. For one thing, I'm not supersensitive any more. Things fly off my back like dust in the wind – that phrase is from an old song—I can't remember who did it anymore. I wake up and laugh every day. Have I got perspective! I feel good—do my yoga exercises every morning, walk for half an hour with my friends, and I'm still dancing three times a week. Also, I don't care so much if I get my own way. I'm so laid back it's a joke. Sex? That's the best. It took me a long time to have a really great relationship with a man, but never say never. My friends seem more and more dear as each day passes. Creativity is not age-limited, I'm here to tell you, and what a joy it is. Don't ever be afraid of getting older. It's so interesting. What will happen tomorrow? How will I meet loss with grace? How will I age with a self that gets larger and larger? So large that you can come inside anytime and have a special space to grow to be whoever you want to be.

Journal #22: Answer an open-ended question.

How are women "new aging"?

(Autumn, 1996)
I've been studying how women age
These days we do it well.
Wrinkle out from wisdom
spread into space
Stride to where we want to go
in our boots – tossed out the heels.
I've been watching how women age
with gusto with Gaia
sky clad at solstice
backs straight on mountain paths
grey hair in beds that bounce
spotted hands that hold the earth
I've been thinking how women age
well

Age is something that doesn't matter, unless you are a cheese.

Billie Burke

Silver Fox Tip

Remember the girl you were before you turned ten. In what ways would you like to be like her again?

Silver Fox Tip

Be a pleasure revolutionary. Think of ten things you've always wanted to do. Choose one. What's stopping you? Do it!

My Ten Things

1) Take a French course in Paris.
2) Hike in the Andes to Machu Picchu.
3) Take a road trip through Newfoundland.
4) Visit the Galapagos Islands.
5) Become a television host for fabulous seniors.
6) Volunteer as an E.S.L. teacher in other countries.
7) Gain fluency in French as well as pleasure by living in France for some months.
8) Sell my condo and live in a quiet but stimulating place outside Toronto.
9) Take a cooking course in Tuscany.
10) Write a book of linked mystery short stories.

It is a mistake to regard age as a downhill grade toward dissolution. The reverse is true. As one gets older, one climbs with surprising strides. George Sand

The afternoon knows what the morning never suspected.

Swedish Proverb

-12-
Body Talk

○ ○

If I had a son, I should say to him: "Beware of women who love neither wine nor truffles nor cheese nor music."

Colette

"I don't know if I should cut them," I cried.

"Cut them!" pronounced the arrogant popinjay at the next station.

"I wouldn't do it if I were you," said his dowdy client.

I stared into the mirror, hyperventilating just a little. Joanne, my stylist, asked me, "What are you really worried about?"

"Whether I should let Peter back into my life." I replied without thinking.

She smiled. "Maybe this isn't the best time to decide. We can cut your bangs next time if you still want to. You know, I can guess where a woman is at in terms of love by what she does with her hair. If she starts growing it, she usually wants a man in her life. A short spiky cut with orange highlights—leaving her husband for a woman. A medium bob—she wants to be safe from out-of-control sex. The mousy over-fifty cut—the woman has given up thinking of herself as sexual."

Hair matters! I am more aware now of how I express myself through my hair. (I didn't cut my bangs; I didn't let Peter back into my life.) And nowadays I dress to communicate my true self and to celebrate my luck at being embodied for this lifetime. I love the beautiful jewelry made by two silversmith friends and the birthstone ring my daughter, Rachel, made for me. I had only known of the milky opal, and that orange-fire opal ring expressed my self-image, more fire than milk. Style matters!

I don't dress up anymore because of someone else's needs. When I was young, I resisted my mother's wish to put me in nice little outfits. I requested only books for my birthdays. I wore my dad's tailor-made tweed skirts and jackets to high school, to the contempt of the popular girls. But later, in my twenties, I began to adorn myself for men, often suffering in tight shoes and girdles. These days my appearance is no longer a commodity. Is yours, and for whom? Or have you gone the other way, and have quit adorning yourself?

The women in Paris were role models for me. I admired their clothes, their walk, and never saw a bad hair day on the streets of Paris. Here's the skinny on French women: they eat intelligently, dress for the theatre of the street, and have taste and knowledge in matters of wine and cheese and décor. They inspired a feminine self I had never dared to allow myself to have. Now, once I arrange that little scarf, I stand straighter, walk like a woman instead of a locomotive, and enjoy flaunting the cool cardboard hat bought in the *Marais* in 1994, the violet low-cut fine wool sweater from rue Bonaparte, and the eau de cologne, *Charlotte,* purchased on *rue des Rosiers* (advertised as the *parfum* of Jeanne Moreau).

The French have a saying that comes from an old torch song: *Regret nothing—in matters of love and food.*

When I lived in Europe I was never hungry, even though portions were small compared to those in North America. The produce was good and comparatively inexpensive—local, not genetically modified, not factory farmed, often organic. Attention was paid to food—by ordinary people at home, by restaurant patrons and the chef, by my friends, by me. Attention is a form of love, and so we were nourished.

Passion was there at the table. I didn't need a man that year.

Being comfortable with hunger can allow us to realize that it's okay to long for delicious food as well as for intimacy, sex, true self-expression. In our lands of plenty, many of us have a greedy relationship with food (often born from a sense of dissatisfaction and a yearning for connection).We don't need to deny these hungers. They give us information and the chance to satisfy needs. We don't have to mistakenly stuff ourselves to feed emotional starvation.

Before we can love well, we have to be at ease with ourselves, have to really live in our bodies. That means feeling our emotions. And we avoid that—through drugs, shopping, alcohol, books, nasty gossip. There so many ways to abandon ourselves.

When we can actually experience painful feelings in our bodies, we can turn our suffering into compassion for ourselves and others. We have within us the power to transmute pain into caring, and thus to overcome what we have suffered, but we can only do that if we can feel our pain.

I've mentioned my difficulty feeling grounded. My one detailed astrology chart displays air in almost every astral location. To come back to earth, I have learned to lean against a tree, my spine against its spine, my heels into the ground, toes up, completely letting my body trust in the leaning. Sometimes I put my palms flat on earth, and wait until I feel balanced. In the Canadian winter I use the earth of a potted plant.

My main escapes are books, especially mysteries, films (the sigh of relief when I settle down with a DVD, by myself), that same old conversation with friends, romance, shopping, and wine. When I travel, I find it harder to avoid direct experience.

In a foreign place I need and want to be continually "awake",
aware of my surroundings.

To return to my body I write, dance, hike in the woods,
and choose, whatever the risk, true connections with friends,
family, a lover, work, and myself. Our bodies talk to others in
ways we can't control, sending messages of our physical and
emotional health or disease. The more we are conscious of
what vibrations we emit, the more we can decipher a man's
body language.

Stress can render us sad and unattractive. Where is stress
manifested in your body? What realistic or completely crazy
ways could you let go of tension? I have many devices. When I
can't sleep, I rock back and forth on my bedside rug. Sometimes
I imagine that a maternal maple tree is holding me and I can
relax into her loving arms. When I have a massage, I imagine
fingers working in hard but malleable butter rather than in my
knotted muscles.

How do you hurt your body? We all are self-destructive
at times, and we usually know what we are doing, but don't
care enough to stop. You don't have to suddenly stop your bad
behavior. You can become aware of your unskillful actions—
aware, just observing. It's a first step to treating yourself well.

You can write in your journal about living the way you
ideally wish to live. Whether it's stopping smoking or eating
more healthful foods or losing weight, you can use my recent
self-hypnotic writing as a model: *Today I'm feeling really
good. I'm doing my exercises to an old Judy Collins tape
and enjoying them. Breakfast is delicious—I actually prefer
oatmeal, organic yogurt and fresh fruit to a chocolate biscotto,
cigarette, and three cups of coffee. I just put on my new outfit,
a long brown silk boho skirt and rust-coloured cotton jersey
with that flattering neckline. I'm looking good, feeling great,
and happy with myself.*

Writing can make us aware of what we're actually feeling. We write to acknowledge what we are really thinking and wishing and needing. We write to discharge blocked physical energy. There is a release when we put truth on paper. Our stories seem to be coming through us rather than our making them up. We can trigger our physiology by writing. Depending on what we are writing, we can get a headache, get high, or get turned on. We can shift from stuck to flow. We can exercise or dance or meditate, and see what happens if we write immediately afterwards.

Make your journal into an extension of your physical body, just as your house can be an expression of who you are. Move your pen from your whole self.

Another way to achieve balance is through the breath. Take three slow deep breaths, and tune into what you are experiencing at a given moment. What we all yearn for is the experience of being alive. Superficial breathing allows us to live half alive, half numb. Once you fully inhabit your body, you begin to live differently. You refuse to be in relationship with others who do not wish to truly know you.

When I was caring for my mother after she became demented and angry, I was hysterical for a while. I dumped my anguish, for her and for me, on friends and family and counselors, being careful to spread out my uncontrolled trance-talking as much as I could. My three ways of returning to my body were being able to talk to a wonderful social worker at the Toronto Alzheimer's Society, writing fast and literally furiously in my journal, and dancing.

I knew that I had to dance. I had always been self-conscious about dancing, partly, I think, because my mother was the dancer in the family and I was told that I took after my *klutzy* father. I joined the Nia (an exhilarating movement system featuring jazz and modern dance, martial arts and body aligning techniques) dance class at the church down the street, and danced into my body. Along with journaling and talking to caring people, it moved me to a place where I knew that I would never abandon my mother, *and I would never abandon myself.*

Dance is full of stories: our dreams, failures, triumphs, and fantasies. We can meet our genuine feelings and voice though a dynamic combination of free writing and dance. As with other meditative and ecstatic practices, both writing and dancing are paths to mindfulness. Dance can free your writing, and writing can inform your dance, your literal dance and your dance of life. There is an interconnection between dance and writing. You are listening to your body, listening to yourself, listening to your words, knowing you have the right to write who you are right now, to dance yourself into self-acceptance. Write your dance, dance your words.

There are so many ways to fully be in our bodies. I suggest you choose those with meaning and joy for you.

And don't forget this one. Look for and accept a man who finds you irresistible.

That's easier to do if you can accept your own beauty. It took me a long time to accept that I am beautiful. I'm not using the word to suggest I look anything like a movie star. But I have finally accepted that I have some kind of beauty, and I can see beauty in almost every woman that I know. The ideal of beauty varies in different times and societies, so we may as well assemble our own appreciative construct.

Love the body you have. Ask your body what it needs. Listen to the whisperings of your blood and flesh.

I've had a great old age because of plenty of chocolate, butter, and young men.

Beatrice Wood, famous potter working
until she died at 105

Journal #23: Be Here Now exercise. Dance for fifteen minutes, and then do a writing meditation, noting what you see, feelings, sensations, sounds, thoughts, reflections, all as they come and go, and in no particular order.

(June, 2007) Feeling my bum on the cold floor. The Brazilian drumming like a close heartbeat. Mom's bracelets moving as I write, inspiring me to dance, remembering her dance. She was so gifted, the star of the Chai group she performed with. Now that's she's dead I'm free to dance well. Pens scratching, the bracelets clinking, the church dog barking, my breath sighing. Weird day. Computer shop a modern rung of hell. What a great time in my life. If I could deal with perpetual anxiety, I would be happy.

Dancing is just discovery, discovery, discovery.

Martha Graham

Journal #24: Hunger – What do you do when you need to fill up the black hole?

1) *Artur has his piano. I play my sonatas on the stove.* Nella Rubinstein
2) *I drank, because I wanted to drown my sorrows, but now the damned things have learned how to swim.*   Frida Kahlo
3) *One more drink and I'd have been under the host.* Dorothy Parker

So it happens that when I write of hunger, I am really writing about love and the hunger for it...and then the warmth and richness and fine reality of hunger satisfied...and it is all one.

M.F.K. Fisher, *The Gastronomical Me*

Silver Fox Tip

"See" your body from the point of view of an onlooker. Then by a lover who adores you. Notice which parts of your body you are intimate with and which you are disassociated from.

-13-
Lovely Lust

○ ○

Wild Women Don't Get the Blues! Ida Cox

What is erotic for you? What stops you dead in your tracks, brings you to your knees, makes you go blind?

Erotic comes from the Greek word *eros,* meaning passionate, wild, energizing love. After Psyche stole a glance at her lover, the god Eros, against his injunction to never look at him, he said, "It's over, baby" (or words to that effect). She was devastated and asked herself, "What must I do to have this kind of love again? What am I willing to do?" She went to Aphrodite (Eros' mother) for help, ready to do whatever she had to do to have great sexual love.

We can look at sexual love as the integration of Psyche and Eros. We can ask ourselves what work we are willing to do to have that kind of thrilling and heartfelt love.

For me, *eros* is also passion for life, the glorious energy that informs our work and relationships when we are fully alive. We find joy in our vital bonds to others and the world, in our longing to taste fleshy fruit, perhaps forbidden fruit, in our daring to have fantasies. We delight in an insuppressible ageless dirty mind.

What else do I find erotic? Erotic is the black lace thong I bought in Paris (to match the wildly expensive bra), the buttery *palme d'or* from the patisserie two doors down from the lingerie shop, his buttery inside thigh.

Is writing sex good for having sex? If you can sustain intensity in erotic writing, you are less likely to tamp down energy in lovemaking. If you can let go in bed, you are more likely to write without inhibition. You are opening yourself to mystery, unpacking shame from repression. You are taking rose satin sheets from the old trunk in the basement up to your bedroom, and letting them air. Your erotic writing could call to mind childhood sexual fantasies, the films or books or boys that excited you, how you learned about sex.

The erotic gives you power. Write from your pussy, write from your clit, write from feelings coursing through you. Write from your love of food, dance, children, yourself, your body, your life work. Write from your sadness. Write from your joy. Be specific and vulnerable. Say what you are embarrassed to say, even to yourself. Reveal specific details, remembered emotions, the messy as well as the fabulous.

What is the sexiest image that ever popped into your head? Where on earth did it come from? I recall the sexual charge I got from Michael playing the master. I was dressed in a maid's costume and placed in different positions, none of them feminist!

And today? What turns you on? What turns you off? What are your ideal situations, positions, recurrent fantasies, frustrations? When your pleasure is in your own hands, what have you learned about your sexual self? If you are in a sexual relationship with a man, what does his lovemaking reveal about him?

Most of us find it difficult to talk about sexual problems and dissatisfactions with a partner. But once you own your sexuality, you can't shut off awareness of disappointment. It takes courage to be honest, gentle, humorous, reassuring. It takes a sense of silliness to mess around without performing.

And it takes a high level of caring, for oneself and for him, never to fake pleasure. Alan Ginsburg said, "You don't have to be right. All you have to do is be candid."

If you have been burnt by love, and are terrified, I certainly understand that. I have retreated several times from the amorous arena, once into a fetal position under my bed covers. But one day you might again believe that love is worth the pain. You don't have to rush into anything. You could wait until you trust yourself, the relationship, and the man before you sleep together, even if it takes many months, even if it takes years. If he won't wait, then screw him (actually, the opposite).

I have to feel safe before I can sleep with a guy. First, I need to feel adored. Next, in order to feel secure and relaxed, I ask him to take an AIDS and STD test and to show the report to me. By the time I have responded to his sexual invitation with my counterproposition and then we wait for the results, enough time has passed for me to begin to know the man. On two occasions a potential lover has passed those health tests, yet I found I couldn't sleep with him. Not because he wasn't a good person, even a person that I liked and esteemed, but because I could see the end before we began and so couldn't begin.

What if you do see the end before you start, and you start anyway? You certainly don't have to follow my approach. If both you and the man want a fling, or a fuck buddy, or a fine but limited romance, why not? Perhaps you have more courage than I to go for who turns you on, eschewing the safe and expected. Why not relish spontaneous forays into the world such as prelude dinners with dashing men whom you might never see again? Why not flirt and dance? Why not play, and if you wish, play around?

I can't play around, for reasons of intensity, but the downside of the way I, and many other women, operate is that we can spend years in a relationship, years that might be better spent on ourselves (with an occasional lover when we want him). Maria, a painter I met in Mexico said, "All that time I wasted on men when I could have been painting. There was some pleasure, and some meaning I guess, but no relationship has given me what my art has."

Serious serial monogamy has been my way, but in my next life maybe I could be a female libertine. Perhaps the double standard will be gone by then, and we will have shed internalized rules of the patriarchy. Think of it! No more sexual guilt; no longer judging our freer sisters.

Even though I haven't been promiscuous, I have done crazy things when all I could think about was sex with a certain someone. Driving for eight hours in a blizzard to see him. Finding the earring on the floor of his bedroom, and letting myself believe his excuses. Obsessing about his eye for other women. Every room I entered with him, every time, I checked to see if there were women more attractive than I. Crazy, crazy, crazy in a way I'd never been before. And, thank goodness, have never been since.

I'm older now. We older women have learned some things. We are better at emotional sexual expression, better able to speak the language of love after all our years of stumbling toward true communication. As well, we aren't as preoccupied with results, and we aren't driven by our waning hormones.

That doesn't mean that we are not thrilled by physical connection. Many women over sixty or seventy or eighty report that sex is better than ever before.

There *is* fever in the evening.

I like to wake up feeling a new man. Jean Harlow

Journal #25: *What I want in sexual love. What I can live without. What I must have.*

(A **Write**, October, 2006)

I want a great sexual love. What do I mean by sexual love? A primal connection with another. A mutual adventure to the mysterious underworld where we have the power to fly. The magnetic pull to keep touching each other, emotionally and physically.

I must have that connection or I'd rather not have a lover. I can live without my preconceived ideas of who I want to be with, as long as I can feel that inchoate bond.

Is it realistic to think in terms of heart's desires? I think it would be unrealistic to deny the reality of the heart. I was taught to deny that reality, to narrow my horizons, to be sensible. Now that I'm 63, I don't want to be sensible, I want to kick up my hardened heels and dance to whatever music thrills me. Why not? Why live in a small box when the large, if sometimes scary, world is out there?

Journal #26: *List 3 erotic fantasies: 1) a sexual experience you would have, 2) one you would have only under certain conditions, and 3) one you would have only in your imagination.*

1) I once wanted a man to fuck me wearing a *tallis* (if I were Catholic I'd want to make it with a priest).
2) I am in a luxurious private car on the Orient Express with two sexy witty men, both desperately wanting to ply me with champagne and indefatigable attention.
3) This one stays in the privacy of my imagination.

There is only one big thing—desire. And before it, when it is big, all is little. Willa Cather

There is nothing safe about sex. There never will be.

Norman Mailer

Journal #27: *Compose Three Lovemaking Scenes.*

(Spring, 2005)

1) How did we get to the bed? How did we take our clothes off? Did he undress me? Or I him? How did we start, what did we say, how did we move together? I remember floating, remember orgasm after orgasm, remember his orgasm, remember the unusual peace between us, after. But no details remain, just the feeling of fluidity.

2) I had told him that my boyfriend was coming to town and that I was unavailable. He seemed to accept that but hung out with me anyway. Each evening he would ask what I was doing the next day. "Going to the poetry reading at *Bellas Artes*" I might say, and he would show up, and ask if I wanted a meal or a drink after. "What are you doing with me?" I asked once, "when there are twelve women to every man in San Miguel?" He answered, "I'm happy in your company." I guess I knew that he had a crush on me, but I didn't realize how drawn I was to him until we were sitting at the Maria Muldaur concert, with our shoulders almost touching. Feeling the heat between our shoulders, I pretended that nothing was happening.

3) His skin smelled of wet moss and tobacco and his eyes were a warm hazel. He was tall and lean with sharp planes on his face and a small high butt.

Silver Fox Tip

While journaling, wear a scarlet hat or scarf—the rule is, while wearing it, you can't judge yourself.

When asked at what age women no longer lust, Princess Metternich of Austria replied, "I do not know. I am only sixty-five."

-14-
Fear & Risk

○ ○

I'm frightened all the time, scared to death. But I've never let it stop me. Never! Georgia O'Keefe

Fear was stopping me from taking action. I made a list of all my fears, forty-seven items. None of them came true.

I was alone at a friend's Lake Huron cottage when I realized that I was no longer ambivalent about leaving the husband I still loved. I also realized that I didn't have the guts to leave even though I believed: 1) I could never be the person I wanted to be if I stayed, 2) my then-husband and I would end up hating each other if we stayed together, and 3) it would be better for our children if we separated.

I decided to do one brave thing a day in order to exercise my bravery muscles. Before I could hesitate, I put on my hiking boots and walked to the lilac-scented country road where a big barking Rottweiler had chased me. The dog ran after me again. It didn't bite me. I continued with my bravery exercises for the next months, did everything I was afraid of, confronted people I needed to confront, and volunteered to make all telephone calls to combustible parents at my school. "Just do it," I said to myself.

That decision to develop my courage changed my life. I now know that I can take greater and greater risks, and I do. I can leave sheltered paths for strange and frightening byways if

I need to. Just before leaving my marriage, I entitled a course I was about to teach, *Writing on the Edge.* For that program, I created exercises to explore ways of living bravely and recommended forays to the edge. I have been following my own advice, walking my talk (along some pretty interesting peripheries) ever since.

Many of us make fear-based decisions because we have internalized messages from parents, teachers, the media and the world. We have been conditioned to choose security over freedom. We have been taught to be cautious, careful, obedient, and fearful of failure. Acknowledging and naming our worries—the unnecessary ones, the anxiety-triggered ones—is a first step to standing up to them.

I come from an anxious family. My parents were good people who had had cause to be fearful, and were overly controlling because of their anxiety. I have repeated that pattern with my own children, as well as with my husband and lovers. At times, they have all held up a mirror for me to look at how micromanaging I can be.

When we try to plan out how a relationship should be and how the other should react, when we worry too much about others' reactions and sensitivities, when we make assumptions before checking them out, we are in a lose/lose situation. We are stressed, and others are, at the very least, irritated. As well, we give up the possibility of sharing a problem with another if we imagine what he wants or is thinking. We take on both sides of the relationship, and at those times we are having a relationship (and a crummy one) only with ourselves.

The less free-floating anxiety we have, the less we try to impose control. The less we project fears into the future, the more we can risk. For many of us over 50, the perception of less time left increases our willingness to risk. The more we risk, the more we're truly alive.

A New Age prescription I have followed suggests that whatever excites you will draw your dream nearer. If the excitement is fear-based, then you will draw what you fear into your life. Even if your excitement is positive, doubt can block your desires.

A lot of us are imprisoned by worry—of losing what we have, of not getting what we want. We fear losing status, looking ridiculous, being overlooked. Many women have a secret nightmare of becoming a bag lady. But if we can stop clinging to a life we find narrow and constricted, there's a chance of new possibilities.

Of course there are times when fear can be useful. It can energize you, heighten your awareness in the face of danger, give you fast information for avoiding that crash on the highway, for escaping a rapist. Fear can foster vigilance when warning signs appear at the beginning of a relationship. Fear can engender greater consciousness, the ability to protect yourself and to choose your own circumstances.

Many women avoid a committed relationship later in life because of, among other reservations, the fear of becoming a caregiver. A new love, no matter how strong the connection, just can't carry the same depth of attachment as a mate of many years. That risk is real, that fear a legitimate concern. Nevertheless, it could rob us of the joy of true love.

We can create more positive beliefs through journaling. We can design strong intentions to go after what we want. We can allow ourselves to put down embarrassing apprehensions, and then read the dissonance between worry and *what is*. When we are confronted with our own fear-filled fantasy life on the page, we can slowly begin to gain courage.

There are acronyms for FEAR: Fantasized Experiences Appearing Real; Future Empowerment Awaiting Resolution; False Expectations Appearing Real. After making my list of fears at the Lake Huron cottage, I noted my concerns about future love and then rewrote them as positives. To replace my fear of never having love again, I wrote, "There is at least one man out there for me." I replaced my fear of being too old for men to want me with, "Men seem to like me right now, and I'm not exactly young." I needed to resist my tendency to avoid failure in love. After my first lover dumped me to return to a former girlfriend, I decided to enter a relationship only if the guy loved me more than I loved him and spent a good part of my twenties limiting the possibility of happiness to prevent the prospect of being hurt.

Trust is the goal. The choice to trust is like choosing to let go of a trapeze in order to grab the next rung—you need to tolerate the uncomfortable gap. You need to believe that it is worth it to let go of what you have in order to gain your heart's desire. You need timing and faith to make the leap. It's not easy to bear those few seconds between bars. But until you can let go of the familiar trapeze, you won't be ready to grasp the waiting one. Confidence is the only way to release our lives from fear. It allows us to stop clinging to the apparent safety of the past with whitened fingers. It gives us the choice (that must be made over and over) to soar into an unknown but potentially richer future.

Unable to bear the chasm between the old and the new, we often deny, or rationalize. We hold tightly onto our small unloved trapeze bar, not realizing that we are frozen by our own thoughts, that what we call safety is generated by beliefs that block us. It feels safe, the bar that is ours. There are women who dislike their jobs and could retire but fear the void. Some of us dislike old friends, but still convince ourselves we want something from them. Others could leave a dead marriage, but are afraid of a reduced lifestyle, or the misery of separation and divorce, or punishing anger from husband, children, or others.

"Always do what you are afraid to do," Ralph Waldo Emerson's visionary Aunt Mary advised him. What are *you* afraid to do?

It is life near the bone, where it is sweeter.

Henry David Thoreau

Journal #28: Name a fear that affects your being able to love. Design a product to exaggerate your problem.

Chronic anxiety. (February, 2006)   The anxiety anklet! This sterling silver chain anklet, with two charms – a worried face and a tangle of silver wire – will guarantee depth in your unreflective life. Your shallow happiness will be enriched by a motif of misery. Seven out of ten people found that by wearing this anklet for only five days, their lives changed for the worse and they felt the better for it.

Journal #29: A slam is an event in which poets compete within the strictures of word and time limits.Write a poem in 10 minutes using three words: wound, barricade, sharp.

Can you collect stones
To barricade beating
        fluttering
            winged feelings
against the wounding winds
If you gather enough pretty stones
enough rocks from memory-laden places of joy
can you protect your self
from being hurt again?
This stone in my hand
sharp amethyst quartz
ribbed by narrow lines
the colour of subtle
will it ward off the spirits
that feed on heart tissue?

Silver Fox Tip

If you knew for sure that you would not fail, imagine what you could do.

The worst things in my life never happened. Mark Twain

-15-
Ambivalence

○ ○

I feel the ambivalence in everything and it is frightening, and so I try to deal with it through my work. I try to visualize it and to express the fragile centre between extremes.

Louise Bourgeois

I asked an attractive friend whether she was ever ambivalent about her lovers. "Always," she snorted. "It starts with the first hello."

After a certain age, can commitment come without ambivalence?

I don't know the answer to that question. I do know women who confessed that even as they were walking down the aisle in their fifties (in two cases, sixties), they were thinking, "*What* am I doing?" I know women who swung back and forth for years before committing to a man. I know women who say they want a man but put up road blocks to a relationship. And I know women who say they want a man in their lives "someday" but not "today".

I can't imagine being in mid-life or later and not having some ambivalence about involvement with a man. We know too much. We're survivors of difficult relationships, or a terrible marriage. Or perhaps we had a wonderful marriage and we know too well that a lover can die, that loss is truly possible.

Many of us find that we're ambivalent about a real relationship with a real guy. Perhaps the most troubling is the question, "What am I going to have to give up?" We fear that we will lose ourselves. We are terrified of becoming half of a couple, the appropriated half. In my case, freedom is more important than status, money, companionship, going to more dinner parties, or whatever a man might provide. Freedom is even more important than sex. Perhaps love will trump my extreme need for freedom, my deep fear of being trapped.

For many years after my marriage ended, I wanted a love but I didn't want a partner. I didn't want to consult, share, or compromise. I didn't want another parental figure in the house after I'd reached a pleasant way of living with my teenage daughter. Although I sometimes missed being with someone with whom I was passionately in love, I felt fine almost all of the time. I remembered reading a study suggesting that unmarried women were the happiest in North America.

During most of my post-divorce years, I haven't been willing to create a lasting love. I did find true temporary love a couple of times. There was real caring, on both sides. But I wasn't ready for anything more than I was ready for, and perhaps neither were the men I chose and who chose me. I was chronically ambivalent about those men. After the first months, the internal dialogue would start—should I stay or leave? It was awful to be stuck. Sad being half-hearted.

Have you found yourself in that place? At a crossroad, and the air is too thin. Your breath is shallow, and a panic attack waits at the roadside. He's too good to leave, but not good enough to keep. Have you experienced the discomfort of waiting to take action until there was clarity, to hang in there with doubt or confusion, to wait until the mind and heart were one? At some point, did you make a choice, and found that making a choice brought back power? Even if you made what looked like, what could have been, a mistake, you put yourself in charge of your destiny.

In my years of being single again, I had three romantic loves. Peter I loved madly, deeply, anxiously. But I felt that I couldn't leave my daughter, my friends, my job and apartment and take a chance on a man I couldn't trust.

I loved the other two men, Anton and Michael—just not enough.

The day after I fell in love with Anton at the Council of Canadians meeting (and told him that I wanted to see him again—the bravest thing I've ever done), we spent an afternoon walking around Toronto, a six hour urban hike along Queen West. I was high on happiness. But soon enough I became uncomfortable, pressed into more closeness than I wanted.

Every time I travelled, even for a few days, Anton would cut me off emotionally. And whenever I felt hurt by the emotional abandonment, I threatened to leave. It worked. He usually ended his cold withdrawal. But I didn't want to keep doing that—threatening to leave, my default position in any argument, whether stated or not.

I found a journal from my time with Anton in which I listed five conflicting selves, all bickering about who would be boss. That entry reveals some of why I was having love trouble. My introverted self said, "I need my own space." The teenager giggled, "I'm so popular—I love it." My mature self was clear that she would love to have a loving relationship. My aging identity confessed that she was afraid of loneliness. And my adventurer wanted freedom more than anything.

Again I second-guessed myself with Michael. I had met him through a newspaper ad that I placed and was smitten right away. We had a perfect follow-up date a week later, wandering through small art galleries, supper at a charming bistro where we didn't notice that we had closed the place down, so involved with each other were we.

At times I felt close to Michael, an amiable open-minded doctor, but he had made it clear in some unspoken way that I wasn't to expect to see him during the work week, unless he decided on a meeting. Sometimes sex was wonderful. At other times he had problems responding to me. He would often wake me in the middle of the night. "At my age I can't waste an erection."

One morning Michael said to me, "You're the most important person in my life." What a responsibility! I felt that I really didn't know him well enough for that burden, and at the same time resented his compartmentalizing me into The Weekend Girlfriend. I wondered at my losing my temper so often, even though I rarely had done so for six or seven years. Did that mean that what was between us had moved too fast? Or did it mean that the relationship was too hard, and it wasn't right? I was confused.

Ambivalence is the psychological term for a condition in which we consciously desire something we are unconsciously afraid of getting. We work against ourselves, and sometimes stay too long with the wrong partner, and at other times push away the very people who could help us heal, who could love us and whom we could love.

Ask yourself, do I really want a partner? If so, do I want a partner whom I live with or would I prefer a live-out partner? Is the best thing for me right now a sexual friendship? Or is marriage what I dream of? Is it possible that I actually want to be single?

Have you been entering into relationships with hope, as I have, and then fleeing or sabotaging them? I haven't wanted to be with a man whom I haven't truly wanted, or who didn't truly want me and see me as an important love. Yet, unfair as it seems, I felt trapped whenever the man pushed for permanence.

It is possible that I acted ambivalently because the right man hadn't come along, perhaps because I wasn't ready for him. Nonetheless, I kept finding myself stuck. Not a happy situation, for me or for the men.

On the other hand, each man has known where I stood (at just about any given moment!). I wonder if any of them were ready for total allegiance. If they had been, why did they stay with me? Why didn't they give me an ultimatum?

Ambivalence can come when we are not sure whether we're afraid to commit because he is investing so little in the relationship, or whether he's holding back because we're lukewarm. Is it him, or is it me?

How can that be sorted out?

I used to believe that I wasn't giving mixed messages. I only used the word *love* when I believed I could commit. I have said *I'm in love* but closed my mouth tightly on saying *I love you,* except to my husband and two of my lovers. A friend of mine who lived in Paris had a lover who kept saying, "*Je t'aime beaucoup.*" She thought, "He must really, really love me." She didn't realize that *je t'aime* is the real thing, and that *je t'aime beaucoup* only means I like you a lot. When I say *I love you*, I mean commitment. *I'm in love with you* means I am really into you and let's see what happens. But to another of my friends, *I love you* means I want to sleep with you and *I'm in love* means I really adore you and I will cut you a lot of slack.

How to be clear? I've been learning not to give mixed messages and I don't fall for anyone anymore who messes with my mind, whether deliberately or not. If I want to know his intentions, I ask! To know my own intentions, I request information from a dream, help from a friend or therapist or myself by using a divination device or my journal.

Use your journal to ask for guidance. The very act of asking for help and then writing opens us to our own inner guidance.

You can pretend a decision has already been made to help you in making a decision. Humour helps. So does courage. It's a brave woman who can admit that it's she who is commitment-phobic. So much easier to blame it on him. And him. And him.

Once you are tuned in to your real feelings, once you have realized what you really want, then stay or leave. If you decide to leave, don't hesitate, don't second-guess yourself into settling for half a love.

Usually when we are stuck, ambivalent, worrying about what to do, we already know, already have the answer, we just don't want to face it.

We do not know enough to be pessimistic. Rilke

Journal #30: Write about a time of ambivalence.

(Summer, 1990) I am walking in the land of the dark grey clouds. I can't breathe. I keep swallowing my truth and Saint John's Wort. I'm apologetic about my life although it looks okay, even to me. Yet I know I'm not aligned with the shiny moving particles of meaning.

A hike yesterday with the Bruce Trail Club. Then a dip in a cold river (stood fixed up to my thighs until a man—Peter—said to me, "Think white instead of icy water, dive into white." At the Caledon Inn supper I spoke with several interesting people, including Peter. I have this intimation that he will be important in my life. That I could love him. And that he could love me. So that's pretty exciting, but I'm also agitated because I don't know if he will call.

Do I want him to call? I have been contented without a man.

Journal #31: What have I been telling myself by telling my story?

(Summer, 2002) That I want to live alone, and have a love that is convenient, on my terms, in my bed when I want, but not in my way when I want to write. That I'm scared of love, that I doubt it would bring me happiness. That I know I've been passive, and want more and more to become a player in my own life. That I think writing is a way for a woman to enlarge her life, to hear herself, and have a chance to do something about her situation.

I am not prepared to be a partner. No wonder I keep turning up guys who won't negotiate. Only when I become ready to work with another, ready to see another's point of view, ready to compromise, will I be able to draw a partner to me.

Sometimes we tell our stories in the guise of fiction. I wrote a short story that reveals my own issues without my realizing it until after it was published. Here are some excerpts:

◆   ◆   ◆

What would I do with my life if I didn't get Mark? How could being a part-time librarian, shopper, mother, and friend be enough? Beneath my apparent autonomy, I secretly believed that without a husband I'd just be putting in time until I died.

◆   ◆   ◆

Writing was giving me a high. The words seemed to come through me rather than from me, and I loved the way ideas and memories rushed from the corners of my mind to connect in surprising sentences.

I loved the character of Chloe, my murderess, a brave woman trying to find herself through volunteer work and homicide.

It didn't take long before I had to write every day, or I felt edgy, guilty almost. And there was pleasure in not knowing exactly what was going to happen, or what Chloe or the other characters would do. I was finding out what I was thinking by writing. It was a great adventure, a more elegant game even than therapy.

◆   ◆   ◆

I found the perfect lover in Staff-Sergeant Rogers. His being a Younger Man, his not being Jewish Husband Material, freed me from my conditioned response to men. We took turns playing a homicide officer who sleeps with the chief suspect. Took turns owning the keys to the handcuffs. He was always at the ready, always up for anything, always totally into me. But, best of all for a writer, shift work kept him from being underfoot.

(This ending is a pretty clear message of my real thinking about men at the time.)

Silver Fox Tip

Hang with your ambivalence until one day you wake up and know what to do.

We don't see things as they are, we see them as we are.

Anais Nin

-16-
Anger

○ ○

I was so angry I almost said something. Unknown

There is a photo of me at three years of age, glowering, hands
on hips, wearing my favourite bicycle-patterned dress. I was
a child who was allowed, even encouraged, to have tantrums.
I think it made my parents feel more alive. I was never sent to
my room. As a mid-life adult, I had to teach myself to leave a
situation when I could feel the aura of anger coming on. I had
to metaphorically, and sometimes physically, send myself to
my room.

During my marriage I believed I had a right to be angry,
and a right to express myself by yelling, especially when I
had PMS. I thought I was strong when I yelled. I thought the
object of my fury could hear me more clearly the more I raised
my voice. I didn't understand that acting out made me weak
and strident. I didn't realize that I made myself not-hearable. I
didn't get what I really wanted—connection, understanding.

When my son was ten, he told me how scared he was by
those tantrums. He explained that when I apologized afterwards,
explaining my pre-period state, which he remembered my
doing when he was five years old, he thought that PMS "was
something that made you yell, and not remember that it was
me standing in front of you." He told me that he'd decided that
he would never marry a woman with PMS.

Click! I understood that I wasn't a person who was able to express anger in a healthy way, as I had imagined. I had been terrifying an innocent child whom I loved. At that moment I decided to stop the yelling. At first, I managed to reduce it. Now, and perhaps this has as much to do with being post-menopausal as with maturity, I almost never feel a need to yell.

Several years later, when I was working on our settlement agreement with my ex-husband, I became fully in touch with the extent of my fury. I was in a rage almost all the time, and kept it burning by talking to friends who supported my rage. I would phone fifteen friends and ask, "Am I crazy or is he?" (There was only one right answer.)

Then one day I thought about how much time I had been angry throughout my marriage and that one of the good things that could come out of a painful separation was the space and motivation to deal with my anger and channel it. With the help of a book by the extraordinary Vietnamese monk and social activist, Thich Nhat Hanh, I did moderate my anger. During the year I taught in Europe, I was lucky enough to be able to hang out in the presence of Thich Nhat Hanh at his monastery in southern France. I learned even more from his gentle but tough ways than I had from his wonderful books.

Here's a valuable anger meditation I learned from him: Breathe, noticing your breath, acknowledging your anger, not denying your anger, but not feeding your anger. Don't talk or write about the other's "badness". Don't keep going over and over what was done to you. Breathe mindfully for five minutes, or five hours. Breathe until you are calm. Breathe until you shift from being beside yourself to being yourself again. Now you have options. Now you can decide what you wish to do.

I have spent time at many meditation retreats and have become more mindful. I took conflict mediation courses, and became the mediator at my school and in my co-op apartment building. Books on anger, a therapist, and my journal all helped.

One of the journaling exercises I did, to try to understand my ex-husband's point of view, was to imagine a dialogue that went like this:

ME: Why didn't you care about my needs?
HIM: I did, more than for anyone before, but you kept pushing your needs at me. .
ME: But you wouldn't hear me
HIM: You never asked for anything nicely. You were always yelling, pounding away at me.
ME: I did ask for things nicely at first. When you wouldn't hear me, I attacked.
HIM: Well, you scared me. I loved you, but you terrified me....

Meditating, cognitive therapy, writing can free us from crazy anger. But how can we reclaim rightful anger? How to access the power that is fueled by the anger allowed to men in our society? Remember that old saying, "He's assertive, she's aggressive—actually, a bitch."

Here's a plan. Pretend you are an alpha entitled man. Throw off your uncomfortable strappy high heels, your Spanx, your lacey push-up bra that cuts into you. Throw off the conditioning that prepared you to give away power and become a Pleaser. Put on a strap-on dildo over your clothes (in your own place!) and experience how easy it would be to thrust your way into the world.

Or you could revel, smiling like a Cheshire cat with a mouth full of clotted cream, in a nasty retaliatory fantasy. I wrote a story inspired by a man who told me I was uppity, and who begged me to be more feminine so that we could get along. I created an irresistible hetero butch protagonist who tamed the macho man. He ended up begging her to love him.

Another story was triggered by a payback daydream in which I fantasized settling scores with a man who had discarded me by slow painful degrees. I created a goddess-worshipping heroine who wanted to get even with a Member of Parliament who had dumped her by email. She manifested the warrior goddess Diana and organized her friends to form a goddess circle. They prepared for a demo. They contacted all the local media. When the cowardly M.P. arrived home, forty-seven people awaited him, mostly women. My heroine led the chant: DICKIE DICKSTEIN DEADBEAT DATE. The story made the front page in all the papers. There were articles in the Life section of three newspapers, an op-ed column, and an interview on a popular national radio show.

You could also write "an unsent letter" in your journal. Don't swallow your anger! Sear the page with your fury. The kind of salutation I indulge in: *Dear man, you are such a fucking bastard.* Follow with specific details. At the least you can express your anger, and your words are recorded if you later decide on a confrontation.

If you decide to send a very revised version of your letter to the guy, wait until your rage has cooled, and write or speak your truth with an awareness of his vulnerability. It's not only you who are taking a risk when you speak the truth—what's difficult for us to express may also be extremely painful for others to hear.

Sometimes I create an Angry Day. I take a day to wallow in obsessive self-righteous stuff and the clutter of soul-destroying thought-loops. I write, pound pillows, indulge in gossip with a dear friend, belt out songs like "I Will Survive." Then I think about what I can do to best deal with the anger. Try it.

Indulging in the above fantasies and devices are harmless and even important. Most women forgive too easily. Other women remain attached by dull red cords of anger to men they have physically left or who have left them. Feel your anger, wait until you're not in a state, do what you need to do to reach serenity, express your anger safely and compassionately if you wish, and only then, if truly ready, let go of some of it.

Grab the broom of anger and drive off the beast of fear.

Zora Neale Hurston

Journal #32: Write an analysis of a time of anger.

(October 13) Did it again. See it so clearly now. The rage, building up, the fury, the confrontation, the screaming, the drama, the making the other person wrong. My anger is a fat crippled cat, hissing, attacking. Then the mood swing to despair. Then in love again. I'm ashamed. I know I'm bad. Will he still love me?

How to break this pattern? Am I choosing wrong partners? Am I right to be angry, even if I express it horribly? Am I somewhat bipolar within the brackets of normalcy?

My mother told me I had tantrums as a kid. Chemically induced eruptions or desperation to be heard? Or did the desperation affect the chemistry?

Journal #33: What makes me angry is... (a monologue running out of your pen)

(Journal 2007) I almost broke up with Anton when he called up to ask me to turn off the light in the upstairs bedroom. "I can't do this," I thought. "I can't be with someone who thinks I'm a baby, who thinks I don't know enough to turn off the light by myself—I can't be with someone so controlling." By the time I got downstairs, I decided to wait before I dumped him, the guy who had always reminded me of my father—my father who often had accused me of not turning off lights, and didn't believe me when I said I had. You think I'm touchy? I didn't go out on a third date with another guy who kept telling me how to tie up the shoelaces on my hiking boots.

Silver Fox Tip

If you're in a state of anger, allow yourself fifteen minutes a day to indulge in really feeling your fury. Even exaggerate your sense of outrage. Do this every day until you are calm enough to choose a good way of dealing with your anger.

Anger makes us all stupid. Johanna Spyri, *Heidi*

-17-
The Dating Classroom

○ ○

A kiss can be a comma, a question mark or an exclamation point. That's basic grammar that every woman ought to know.

Mistinguett, French actress and dancer

You can learn to date in the way you learned grammar and punctuation. Points, slashes, and marks make a map for navigating syntax. Slow down when you see a comma; stop suddenly for an exclamation point. Similarly, there are signs that help you orient yourself on the dating roads and off-roads. Slow down for a red flag; stop when you see an-accident-about-to-happen.

Most of us can look back to the very early days of a doomed relationship, and remember the clues that we ignored. We wouldn't break grammar rules in an application letter for a job. We wouldn't ignore highway signs. But somehow, if need and greed kick in when meeting a delicious impossible man, we let ourselves head for a crash.

There are dating sign-posts. You can pay careful attention to the first kiss. When you start reading a story, does the first sentence invite you to read on? Does it grab you? Does it take you gently by the hand and invite you into the tale? Similarly, the first kiss can tell you a lot. Are you captivated by his kiss? Do you want more of his thrusting tongue? Or do you prefer tender exploring lips?

A female therapist once told me, "I know everything I need to know about a man the first time we make love." Whether or not you agree, if you are able to keep your wits about you (much harder when the lovemaking is fabulous), you can certainly learn a thing or two about the real man between the sheets.

If you fall in love with the wrong man again, ask yourself what you're doing. Ask: "Does he treat me as if he loves me? Does he treat me with care and respect? Is he present to me?"

But don't (as some of my friends think I have done) hold out for perfection. We'd all prefer to be able to put into practice the potato head theory of dating. That is, to be able to take all the things we've liked from all the men we've known and then attach them to the potato we're presently interested in. But, as many wise women have sighed, "You can't have everything." You have your bottom line, the things you could never accept in a relationship. You have a list of things you want in a man, but perhaps some items are negotiable, such as his being a good dancer or his having the same taste as you in movies.

A warning sign flashes when he wants you, but you don't much care if he's with you or not. Continue on that road to a dead-end. The buzz of the beginning, the pleasure of being adored, the relief at having found a likely boyfriend, all these might carry the relationship for a few weeks or months, and then, for reasons of insecurity, delicacy, or lethargy, you might overstay your happiness.

On the other hand, desperation can make us accept second best or less. You might hook up with a man who realizes he doesn't have to work hard to satisfy you and then rationalize and indulge in enabling fictions. You keep telling your friends that 1) he wants to leave his wife, or 2) he loves me—he just can't say it, or 3) he's really busy at work.

One evening Michael said to me, "If I were ready to commit, I could commit to you. Or I could not." I immediately rationalized, "How many people commit, and then it falls apart? This could go anywhere. He's shut no doors—doesn't even think that way—just knows he shouldn't be, can't be, committing right now. He really likes me." I wanted to avoid facing reality. I stayed with him longer than I would stay with him now.

Unreturned love does not create happy love. Whether one is the more wanted or the more wanting, unrequited love ushers in unsuccessful love.

Once we have thrown out some past baggage, we can think more clearly. We rarely begin a relationship when we realize that one of us likes the other more, that the caring isn't equal. We certainly don't stay in such a relationship. We are ready to be single and content until a very right man is in our sights, or runs towards us across a crowded room on an enchanted evening.

In the dating classroom, we learn that in a long life we will likely have alternating periods of being mated and being single. That knowledge takes the pressure off feeling we have to find someone right away. If not now, another chance will come. As my father used to say, "There will always be another bus if you wait at the bus stop."

Many of us have dated the same man, with different packaging, over and over. It hasn't worked. As long as we keep being attracted to men who are not good for us, men who are not enough different from their predecessors to be able to make us happy, we are stuck in the same grade—whether it's kindergarten or high school, until the lessons are learned. Until then we keep giving the same wrong answers to our relationship questions. We need to study our patterns by doing our homework.

How to do that? Once again, I suggest my personal prescription: journaling, meditation, therapy, and mindful dating.

But how can we actually choose a man more wisely? We can't be attracted to someone we are not attracted to. Attraction is a mystery which might be understood, but can never be willed. One choice could be to settle for a "good man"—stable, decent, perhaps dull. But we are not in love.

If you are reading this book, you likely don't want to compromise. It takes courage to refuse to settle for less than you want, courage to walk away from a dangerous temptation, but it's worth it to go it alone for as long as it takes to find an eligible, like-minded man who wants to share the kind of relationship you want.

That time of bravery can often bring us the good that's secreted in difficulty. We have the chance to learn enough and become confident enough to move to the next grade, or even skip a grade or two. With luck and work and patience we can sometimes sprint to graduate school. Eventually, one fine day, the odds are that you might meet a very attractive and available man. He might be your "same man", but the differences will be enough for a wonderful workable love.

I believe that any woman of our age who really wants to marry, and doesn't have any impossible problems, could meet a decent man who wants to marry her within a year. So many men are always coming on the market, and most want to be married. Most heterosexual men over sixty need a woman more than most of us need a man. If he likes you, if he's happy with you, if you make him feel good about himself, he will quickly want to put you in place. His place.

The mythology of "not enough men" for women of our age is ubiquitous and persuasive, but don't believe it. I have met so many men who were lovely. If I could have been satisfied with a lovely guy who was not *my* guy, I could have been married or partnered long ago. But I'm only interested in true passionate love.

One of those lovely men could be *your* guy.

The important message is that there are so many men around. I was introduced to several men by old friends. Some were old friends who had become single. I became acquainted with others through internet sites and personal ads, as well as in interest groups. And I bumped into some charming guys by the random happenings that occur if you are ready to respond to the unexpected. Most were first dates only, or just a couple of dates, yet they were all good enough (with one exception), and some very fine. Just not right for me. I learned to walk quickly away from someone whom I knew was not a soul mate.

The exception to all those lovely men was the second worst date I ever had. He was so angry at me for something (feminist) I said that he started screaming at me in a restaurant (a former student of mine was waiting on us!). Oddly, the worst date was his cousin, a blind date in my early twenties, who also asked me out for dinner. He didn't pose a single question to me, replied to all my questions in monosyllables delivered in the British accent he had acquired at an Oxford summer course, somehow forgot his wallet, and then blitzed me with imploring phone calls for a year (long before call display and almost as long before I believed I had a right to be "rude." Bad dates can be excruciating, sad, comedic material, and great lessons in the dating classroom. If you've made a checklist of what you're looking for, if you have the guts, you can leave a dreadful date quickly and kindly.

Awareness can be raised by noting down what you want in a man: his attitude to romance and affection, how he treats you, and how he treats the relationship. It's useful to make a wish list of what you prefer in his social, intellectual, sexual, communication, financial, personal growth, and spiritual styles. It might also be wise to make a fatal flaw checklist. What can you not bear in a relationship?

What are your negative assumptions about men? Mine were that men were untrustworthy, could let me down, press my buttons to get me going and then put me down as hysterical, not listen attentively, not interested in really knowing me, and would withdraw emotionally.

Yet when I read over old diaries and love letters, I was overwhelmed at how much I was adored, at how it was I who was always pushing people away.

A sentence from the first canto of Dante's *Inferno* is often quoted as a comfort to those of us who have lived long and lost direction: *In the middle of the journey of life I came to myself within a dark wood where the straight way was lost.* It reminds us that others have been lost in mid-life. A belief for some is that unless one gets lost in the woods, one cannot emerge from the dark into a new way of being. We start to ask ourselves what will happen if we continue on our old relationship paths. We wonder if the man we are with is the best man for us. We face whether we are ready to accept the consequences of our current choices. We question what we really want for ourselves.

In mid-life I began to examine why the same old stuff kept happening to me. Perhaps I believed that I deserved to be with guys who sapped my energy. Or perhaps I only felt valuable if I were of use to a man. I began to accept as true that things happen through me and not to me. I owned that I always ran away (my default position) because I didn't feel loved. I got it that I always chose men who were bright, high-achieving, competent, funny, deeply interesting and angry and lonely and wanting a woman as a support system rather than a partner.

As well as the ability to pick up signals, there are techniques one can learn that are helpful when dating. My most successful pro-active method for meeting men was the ad in the Saturday Globe & Mail Personals section. Writing it (with a little help from my friends!) was fun and useful.

I suggest that you write one. You don't have to publish it. Creating the ad is comparable to writing the "elevator speech", the thirty second talk that communicates the essential nature of a new business, or to composing a back cover blurb to advertise a book. You are focusing and summarizing what you want and what you have to offer in a few lines. Think of this as a classroom exercise that clarifies your goal for you. You don't have to send it out to the world.

I don't like lying and I don't recommend lying about your age. But practicing age avoidance in indirect first contact is a good idea (in terms of jobs as well as meeting men). If you believe that your age might not fit someone's idea of a potential lover, be vague about your age in your ad. If you like each other, you can confess immediately or soon after. You don't have to wait for a year, as I did with Peter. I had made myself younger by one year, and was so ashamed of lying that I bribed my eight-year old twin nieces with chocolate bars to keep quiet about it. When I finally confessed, my long-drawn-out guilt-ridden preface caused Peter to wonder if I were a heroin addict or had been in prison. At what he considered a non-problem, he erupted in barks of relieved laughter.

In addition, own your beauty (everyone has a unique kind of beauty) in the ad.

Here are three examples of ads that I wrote for the time I asked for a man through the personals. (Which ad did I actually use? Answer at the end of the chapter.)

1) SOUL MATE wanted by beautiful mid-life woman, adventurous, interesting, creative and kind. Would like to meet a terrific, grown-up man for a serious and fun relationship. Recent photo appreciated.

2) BEAUTIFUL AND ADVENTUROUS mid 50s woman, 60s values, Jewish (you don't have to be), hiker, writer, teacher, eclectic tastes in reading, music, theatre, seeking wonderful man with whom to co-author a love story. Photo please.

3) ARE YOU THE RIGHT MENSCH for me? I'm 56, kind, interesting, adventurous, socially conscious, very pretty, with wit, warmth, and class.

Here are a couple of other models (modified from real ads):

1) Slut in the kitchen, chef in the bedroom. Woman with mixed priorities (37) seeks man who can make a good omelette.
2) I've divorced a better man than you. And worn more expensive shoes than these. So don't think placing this ad is the biggest comedown I've ever had to make. Sensitive F, 64.
3) Will never get it together by myself. Seeking togetherness with another fellow traveller. I'm over 60—you can be any age as long as diapers are not involved.

You can also find out what you want by finding out what you don't want. For your own clarification, write an "unwant ad". List all the men with whom you have had a significant relationship. Then list five negative qualities for each of them. Circle the words that repeat themselves. Ask for what you dislike.

Mine looked like this:

Wanted: A funny, high-achieving, interesting, self-absorbed, somewhat addicted cute guy, who wants me to be his number one support system rather than a partner.

For further illumination, create your own private advertisement. An ad just for you, from you, FYI. What do you have to offer that could be construed as difficult? Be funny and outrageous, but give yourself the message.

Here's what I could write:

A cute shell-shocked but hopeful sixty-something woman wants to love again but doesn't really know what a good relationship feels like. If you cherish your own space, and are prepared to worship and obey me, please write an unusually witty and wise note, and maybe I'll answer.

If, after vetting the letters responding to your published ad (and you can tell a lot from an old-fashioned letter), you decide to meet someone, don't give your last name, make the arrangement through the internet—a blind hotmail account from your local library, or call him after blocking your number. If you decide to meet him, meet in a public place and allow for no more than an hour (if you like him, you can meet him again, if you don't, it's only an hour).

What about rejection? How often is rejection really real? Isn't what feels like a rebuff usually about timing and the fit? It's usually not about you. It's about mysteriously imprinted criteria. Or about social completion. Or the vagaries of his pre-you life. He only likes women with small breasts, or long legs, or blonde hair, sadness in her eyes, or women who talk a lot or don't talk at all. He's got a girlfriend, is married, or is still recovering from a lost love. He has to concentrate on his thesis, or is about to move to another country. What seems like rejection is based on a random template or an unknown back story.

If you feel rejected, it can hurt. But consider how many times you have "rejected" one or more men that you later regretted not starting something with, perhaps because he was so attractive that you were scared, or maybe he was ready for a closer relationship than you were.

I have come to know my "sore places", the feelings triggered by present circumstances, caused by past experience, and I can now be more detached from hooking into what looks like rejection, whether from a blind date or a lover.

Tchaikovsky called Brahms "a giftless bastard". Fred Astaire was referred to as a "skinny actor who can dance a little". Gertrude Stein submitted poems for 20 years before one was accepted. Stephen King submitted 4 novels and more than 50 stories before one saw print. Many now-famous writers received innumerable rejections.

And what about failure? Do you feel that you have failed in loving? Failed in your marriage? I don't believe in failure any longer. Certainly not as a stop sign. What looks like a failure is often a chance to learn from mistakes and become more skillful in love. Relationships last as long as they last. Things change. Some good relationships sour in the sun, which is not a reason to hide in the dark. Other times, if we could have done it better, we would have. Nothing is wasted if we can learn to love better, forgive ourselves and others, avoid impossible situations, pay attention, and choose hope over despair.

So place an ad, register on internet dating sites, go on group hikes, ask friends and acquaintances if they know anyone for you to meet, brave singles' events, ask that gorgeous man in the art gallery or the coffee shop if he's single. What have you got to lose? On the contrary, a man who hears that you find him attractive will only feel warm towards you, whatever his circumstances, and, by exercising your bravery muscles, you will become more courageous. And you will likely feel proud of yourself, whatever happens.

I hope that the dating classroom will be a good learning environment for you. I hope it will help to fulfill your dreams. But I can only take you so far. You have to get out there.

There is too little courtship in the world...For courtship means a wish to stand well in the other person's eyes, and what's more, a readiness to be please with the other's ways...An undercurrent of surprise and thankfulness at one's good luck.

Vernon Lee, 1904

*Answer to which ad I placed in the personal section of The Globe & Mail. Ad #3. I had many replies, and met Michael.

Journal #34: Jung suggested that we draw men to us who reflect our own male energy, our "animus". List what you dislike in men, and what you find appealing. Draw, name and describe your inner man. Mine is Max. Max is both wonderful and terrible. Write a monologue from your inner man, advising you on dating.

Summer, 2005) Oh, Elaine, Elaine, you don't have to spar with every guy you like. You don't have to test him. And you don't have to let your mind whoosh to thoughts of leaving the minute you're anxious about something. Save your apocalyptic thinking for when it's necessary.

Journal #35: A vision five years from now.

(December, 2002) Elaine opened her eyes to a new day in the most interesting town in Vermont.

"I've made organic Guatemalan coffee," said David, her much younger lover. "Do you want to go for a hike on the mountain after breakfast?"

"I'd love to this afternoon," said Elaine, who looked more beautiful and alive at 60 than she ever had, "but I have to bike down to see the editor at Sisters' Vision of Vermont Press—she has some suggestions for the new novel.

"That's great," said David. "You'll have it done before your kids come to visit. I've never seen kids like a mother so much."

(I wrote this seven years ago, long before my son fixed me up with a somewhat younger guy – named David—who does make me coffee in the mornings.)

Silver Fox Tip

Imagine that you are a Silver Fox on your next date. Wear something silver and smile!

-18-
Romance

○ ○

To love oneself is the beginning of a lifelong romance.

Oscar Wilde

Oh, life is a glorious circle of song
A medley of extemporania
And Love is a thing that can never go wrong
And I am Marie, of Roumania. Dorothy Parker

Have you heard the theory that romance novels are women's pornography? Few of us—only 3% of women, according to a 2008 *Atlantic* article—are into hard porn. We want soft sex, sex with a story, sex within a context of conditions. Romance is what makes us hot. No matter how savvy, how experienced, how cynical we are, there's a tiny Cinderella inside most of us who just wants to fall in love. And we want him to be in love too, madly in love.

Falling in love: a transformation, a trap, a bait for self-destruction, a door to happiness? Falling in love can be a revolution of two—it can alter your life. You might find yourself changing your residence, job, country, continent or even sexual orientation in that delicious seizure that shifts everything, including your idea of yourself.

The classic romantic love story always contains an unattainable love—he is either missing, leaving, dying, dead, the wrong age, class, religion or has unpalatable political beliefs. If the lovers do get together, the story ends. No continuing narrative. No dull everyday crap.

To see an outline of your own romance story, think back to your first crush, and jot down ten boys and men you have liked in "that way". Give your account with each of them a chapter title (eg. "My Search for Love", "He Didn't Even Know I was Alive", "A Mistake I Will Never Make Again"). Some of the motifs in your love life will begin to emerge.

I've wasted so much time and energy in endless love dramas. I've spent a lot of time second guessing myself. *Maybe I'm not ready to marry. Maybe I'm pushing away a good man, just as he's coming closer. Do I have the right not to trust him? Is it myself I don't trust?* I would have better spent my energy on my own creative work.

Or perhaps I didn't waste time. Conceivably, I did exactly what I needed to do at each step of my development. I have learned from each romantic partner. And I have forged several short stories and poems in the fires of rage or grief.

I think there's an analogy between a cult and a romance (let's call it a cult for two). We begin in a state of dissatisfaction or transition. We are ready to revolutionize our lives. We meet or are met by someone/a group that attracts us for reasons we might not understand. We believe that if we join the man or the group our lives will have meaning and there will be an end to our loneliness. In both the cult and the affair, there is often a beginning burst of "love bombing" (an emotional commodity that is given in order to get us to join).

There is always something at stake when we start a romance. We want something. We give something. We gain something. We lose something. We get a buzz. We might receive an important gift.

How do we know whether our romance will lead to love? Is it only a temporary infatuation, Cole Porter's "mock turtle soup or the real"? At the beginning, can we know? We all get high at the start of a sweet romance. Those brain chemicals make us feel so great. Infatuation gives us that first rush, a brief period of mutual uncritical adoration. But infatuation depends on uncertainty, and when the uncertainty goes, that kind of romance goes too.

If a man is not really in love with you, after a while you might find yourself pulled between hope and fear. He will get over his initial infatuation. If he doesn't really care, at some point you will come to understand that you will only be "loved" if you are a certain way. His way. You are headed for a lonely place.

If it is we who keep leaving, dating can become an addiction. There's always the promise of something new, something perfect. If we commit to a love, we have to close the trap door so that we can open another door to something deeper. If we find our love, we have to give up the highs, freedoms, and ego-boosting of romance. There is always a price to pay.

Romance addicts are good at instant intimacy. We want the mood altering high. We want the fix and the fixings (travel, wine, candlelight). We don't really want to know the man—we want to look good with him, have a good time, be adored, indulge in fantasies, thrill to dangers, and then we want to be moving on.

When I'm not in love, I miss the singing in my heart. I have loved being in love. Starry-eyed, I have jumped into the air, landing with a jazzy little dance, whether I was in love with a man, or my colleagues, a new friend, my students, or, finally, in my forties, with myself.

I plunged into love with Peter, the first man I became involved with after my marriage ended. One night I asked him, "Why do I feel safer with you than I have ever felt in my life?" He hugged me tight and said, "It's the same". Every day for months he told me that I was a wonderful lover, that I was beautiful, bright, funny and nice. He did countless small thoughtful things for me, and listened carefully, and loved me. But I believed our romance could only have happened because he was leaving town for another job (he didn't believe that). I was so nuts about him that I began to worry that I was riding high for a crash.

On our last night together, we first said that we loved each other. It was incredibly sweet and sad. We made up some words for what we felt for each other: *hassion, pamish*, a mixture of passion and *hamish* (the Yiddish word for homey). I kept crying throughout the night. Peter said to me, "I thought, Elaine is nice, she wants to go out with me. We'll go out and maybe have some fun before I leave. But you weren't supposed to be *you*."

If I could have lived in the present, I would have been so happy that I couldn't have borne it, but my happiness level was kept down by my intermittent fears of what he might do if I married him. *He might turn terrible right after the ceremony, or fall out of love with me within the first year, play around, take me for granted, and, if he does none of those things, and I am really happy with him, then he might die before I do.*

When I read my post-marriage journals, I can see that I was scared of love. I clearly doubted it would bring me contentment. But it was also obvious that I wanted a great love—a great love that combined closeness and passion with a large amount of space. A few years ago, I realized that ambivalence had rendered me passive. I had been waiting for the "right man" to come along and rescue me (from my mixed feelings).

I decided to become a player in my own life. I would write for the kind of man who would want deep connectedness as well as wide spaciousness. I had long believed that writing was a way for a woman to have a chance to do something about changing her situation. I would help myself grow up and face my own terrors, the ways I had kept love at a distance. I would get clear about what I really wanted.

I would write for Mr. Right.

I had learned by then that even if a romance is meant to last, neither of us could possibly adore each other every minute for the rest of our lives. Romantic love is ephemeral, but it can lead to love. The route may be smooth, or filled with potholes and sharp stones. The pain we feel when the perfect masks drop, the sick feeling in our hearts and to our stomachs, can provoke us to run away. But if we're with the right person, and if we're lucky and wise, we'll stay in the relationship even as we grieve for euphoria departed.

Romance can be an entry to knowledge and growth, a key to where real passion lives. In a vision quest, the initiate goes into the wilderness and waits for a dream or body experience which she brings back to her shaman, who helps her interpret it. In a love quest, she goes into the unknown and waits for signs which she brings back to her therapist, close friend, or journal. The searcher learns more about life and herself.

I remember a wonderful canoe trip with Michael. Days on the lakes of Quetico Park; nights under northern skies. Until he broke up with me again. And again recanted. I was so torn, I didn't realize I was having a relationship with myself. Maybe I was happy with Michael for a time because it wasn't a real relationship. More like a holiday. We were both into each other and faithful, and we both needed space. But although I liked some distance, I was frustrated by his compartmentalizing me. I was the weekend girlfriend. The relationship became static. I became anxious. I became bored. I knew that I would never stay in such a relationship again.

If a woman becomes crazy over a man, once the craziness is revealed and released, she will find the life she has lavished on him available for herself, for creativity, friendship and for real love. If you are not obsessed, a man is a fine creature to have around.

Not being obsessed seems a good benchmark. Obsession is not just some designer perfume—it's a big red flag. Don't keep betting on a guy who doesn't have your best interests at heart. You'll lose both time and self-respect.

Never feel guilty about releasing a "love". Whatever is best for you, will be best for everyone. It's a good idea to say goodbye firmly. If you feel unwarranted guilt, remember the bad things and your differences. Blame him (you can be kind later, you can look at yourself later). One of the things that helped me the most was putting one of Peter's idiotic statements on my fridge door so that I could see it every day. His line, after I had once again begged him to be faithful: "I'll only sleep with other women I don't like."

Note all the things you can do without him; note all the things you don't have to do anymore. Find a new passion. It doesn't have to be a lover.

A sharp knife cuts quickest and hurts the least.

Katherine Hepburn

Journal #36: *Write an unsent letter to a present or past lover (as if in the present), discussing romance.*

(1993, to my then-lover) I'm reading a book about romantic love which theorizes that men and women in the West search for the divine in each other because we have no real access to our souls. While we are in love, we feel whole and the world is bright and meaningful. When we inevitably fall out of love, the world suddenly seems dismal and empty, even though we are still with the same human being who inspired such rapture before.

I don't think I'm searching for my soul through you. I do feel that I'm too happy with you. Although I trust in passion, I don't trust passion for very long. I feel that I'm heading for a crash. What happens when you fall out of love? Will I bore you? Will you turn towards the next person who turns you on?

The question is, do I not trust you because I don't trust myself, because I'm scared to love, or am I right not to trust you?

*Journal #37: A **Write** about romance (find out what you really think about romantic love).*

(April 30) Is it all a fantasy? What do I mean by fantasy? Something negative, something you fool yourself with, something that won't come true, can't come true. Why did I call it a fantasy? Why not think of romance as a blueprint for love? You can't build something different than you've ever built before without being able to imagine it first. What do I mean by something different? A great love, with all its toughness, sparkle, deep engagement, space, and sharp edges— all of it, and the commitment to stay with it.

What do I mean by "in love"? For me, first of all, that I actually care as much as the other person. That I'm happy, scared, okay, terrified, but kind of calm inside. With this man I hardly know, I felt both at home and at sea. Safe, excited and nervous. What if he doesn't want me when we meet again? What if I don't want him? But underneath all the fears, way underneath, is a sense of security. Anyhow, I'm willing to jump into this romance, and that's new for me.

Would I be so interested if I hadn't seen *Before Sunrise* three times? If my mother hadn't died? If his son didn't live in Toronto? If I hadn't reached this time of closeness but non-enmeshment with my former husband. Timing does matter, but means nothing without huge energy connection. It's so different, this thing. I've been seduced by appropriate, good men who loved me. I can't help liking this stranger who writes like a fallen angel.

Silver Fox Tip

Lose your head, but keep your feet on the ground.

Love is a fire. But whether it is going to warm your hearth or burn down your house, you can never tell. Joan Crawford

-19-

Getting over a Broken Heart

○ ○

In the depth of winter, I found there was in me an invincible summer. Albert Camus

We know that one day the pain will pass. We know that it's not the end of our lives. We appreciate that it might even be best for us. Then why is a breakup with a lover such agony? Even if we realize he was not right for us, even if we initiated the breakup, if we loved him at all, we will suffer.

The pain is astonishing, sometimes as sharp as a razor blade, sometimes as dull and long lasting as a chronic physical ache. After breaking up with Anton, who was "close but no cigar", I awoke in the middle of every night for half a year, pinned to the bed by iron grief, my defenses scattered on the floor. All I could do was hold myself. I gave myself nightly Reiki treatments, putting my hands on opposite shoulders, then one hand on the other, over my heart. My hands became a container for my wild sadness. Eventually the pain passed, and I slept again.

I was the physical leave-taker, although Anton had left earlier—emotionally. I knew it hadn't been quite right between us, yet I suffered more over him than I can ever remember suffering for love.

Most of us can look back and see that a difficult time that we didn't fully understand and hated living through was a preparation for becoming more whole. The more pressured the crucible, the more possibility of growth. Perhaps on some level we knew that we needed that crucible. Many things don't just "happen". They are willed into being by us, and our partners, consciously or unconsciously. If a breakup happened, it was inevitable, given the time and the players.

Ritual is one of the best means of getting over a broken heart. Both the practice of writing every day in a journal, and the more traditional daily meditation of focusing on the breath instead of on him help us to not close down. Daily work, regular get-togethers with friends, the weekly tennis game, the morning coffee and paper, the Tuesday therapy session—all these routines facilitate closure. They help us to gradually integrate the past so we can approach the future with less protective armor.

One morning several years ago, I decided to free myself from what I believed was an enmeshed relationship with my ex-husband. I went into the woods and found a branch which I broke in two, asking for a coming apart of the two of us in the best possible way—a loving separation. I thought of everything positive I had learned from him, all the ways he had been great to me. Breathing into my belly, I tossed the two parts of the branch in opposite directions.

Later that day I wrote my intention to move on with my life on the flammable paper that some Buddhists use for a burning ritual:

> I want to sever the connection between us that sucks at our freedom. I can "see" the cord connecting my belly button to his, can "feel" the length of the cord, and can imagine yanking the cord. Whatever threads of positive connection are left will endure. Someday I hope he can be part of my family again.

I lit the paper, and doused the ashes with water in my kitchen sink.

Today (just as much because he wanted it) we have a great quasi-sibling relationship, looking out for each other, laughing together, and, often in tandem, enjoying the company of our children.

Another aid for recovery is making a deliberate decision to enjoy the small pleasures of life. Go out to dinner with friends and don't speak of your sadness. See an absorbing play or film. Have a massage, practice yoga, hike in the woods. Remind yourself that life is precious.

I delight in so many small pleasures: a rosemary-infused bubble bath while Billie belts out the blues, learning French at the *Alliance Francais*, teaching fabulous women at a workshop, Margaritas in Mexico, laughing with my children, the songs of my ravine birds. There is the pure pleasure of dancing in the unadorned church basement near my apartment, walking the Bruce trail awash with trilliums in spring, or cycling on Toronto's many trails.

An attitude of appreciation supports recovery.

Each morning I do "the rituals" (five yoga-like and aerobic exercises that allegedly keep you looking and feeling young—whatever the truth in advertising, they are great exercises and take less than ten minutes to do). I make coffee in my small stovetop espresso maker, and top the dark roast with foamed hot skim milk, spiked with Mexican vanilla and flaked with chocolate. I sip my coffee in bed, a heating pad under my shoulders, Albinoni on the CD player, sunlight through the window, and perhaps the New York Times Book Review. I might start reading an exciting book while eating a black plum. Or finish the lemon *tarte* (I shouldn't have bought the whole *tarte*!).

Time helps too.

So does learning from the relationship. I'm more interested in studying mistakes I made than in gathering grudges about the man's deficiencies. I'm still working on being less reactive. Maintaining balance is a continual developmental task for me. I am learning to be more sensitive to myself and others. I am learning to hold another's moods without fleeing.

Sometimes it's right to leave a relationship and sometimes it's so much better to stay. Since I never know for sure if it's right to leave, all I can do is give my best and act on feelings when they become clear. When I sense that I am not as interested in a man as he is in me, or that we want very different things in life, I can leave much more quickly now, often after the first date. The damage is lessened; disappointment is not the same as heartbreak.

Even in the midst of heartbreak, it has become easier for me to hold all my emotions—anguish and anger and forgiveness and regrets and delightful memories—together. And therefore it has become a little easier to recover from loss.

Journal #38: *Write a poem about the difficulty of getting over a broken heart.*

When I tore out your tiny body
from the bloody strings of my heart
Placed you, a homunculus dressed in good grey pants and a white shirt
in front of your house
to bend down and smell a flower I thought
I was a free woman able to choose my good
over love for the The Man always the same man
you were the best, the scariest, the sweetest
I believed when I left you
I had climbed to a higher level
lifted up my tail at the scent of abuse
I performed an exorcism in my mind
but my mind has a mind of its own and you enter my thoughts
unbent and larger than life

The unendurable is the beginning of the curve of joy.

Djuna Barnes

Journal #39: *Design a funeral for a dead relationship.*

(October, last century)
Dear friends,

We are gathered here today to bury my fantasies of Anton. When we met, we started talking and never stopped. Every weekend we would both say, "I had such a great time with you—again." I felt cherished, beautiful, and mostly happy. I thought he was beautiful too.

Before the relationship began, I was ready for a boyfriend and he thought he was ready for a wife. Neither of us was ready for a true partnership. I felt lonely no matter how much he said he loved me.

I couldn't love him enough at the time. He opened his heart to me and deserved the truth that I almost knew, but didn't want to know. I gave him mixed messages because I was confused and so much wanted to "do love" with him.

I want to thank Anton for all the wonderful times and many hours of happiness. I also want to thank him for holding a mirror up to show me the many ways I denigrate a lover or cross boundaries. I am grateful that he loved me. I loved him too, but I couldn't marry him. I'm not sure why.

Let us bury the idea of Anton and me and I will scatter red and yellow leaves on the grave.

Silver Fox Tip

Borrow a cartload of memoirs from your local library, all written by survivors of shattered relationships. They will constitute another group supporting you on your way to true love.

When you get to a tight place and everything goes against you till it seems as though you could not hold on a minute longer, never give up then, for that is just the time and the place the tide will turn. Harriet Beecher Stowe

-20-
Lost Loves

○ ○

One knows what one has lost, but not what one might find.

George Sand

I was driving home from a Buddhist retreat on the Mass Turnpike. Just as I was passing the exit I used to take to Peter's house, with wings on my Honda, I found myself singing along with an Indigo Girls tape, wailing, "I'm in love with your ghost". So many years after I left the man from Massachusetts, I started crying.

It took me ten years to completely get over Peter. Yet something was wrong from the moment I met him. I wasn't ready for love but didn't know I wasn't ready. I had just left a long marriage. I was in a state of crazy euphoria. I thought I was fine because I was so happy to be free, but my nights were hijacked by insomnia. I took sleeping pills more frequently than ever before in my life.

I met Peter on a group hike a few months after I was separated. I thought he was gorgeous. We couldn't stop talking and laughing as we walked.

The first date was great. I slept with him that evening, a very aberrant rashness for a person like me, a cautious nervous kind of person who had asked my first lover to wear two condoms without telling him that I had also gone on the pill. Peter and I spent eighteen hours together, totally grooving with each other, and then he left, saying, "I have to go and visit my mother in a few days. I'll call you when I get back."

I was furious. Here we had had an extraordinary time together, he was going to be in Toronto for three more evenings before going to Florida, and he wasn't going to make the effort to see me or even phone. "Is this going to be my first one night stand?" I wondered. "At the age of forty-six? Oy!"

I decided I wouldn't see him again if he didn't get in touch before he left. I liked him too much.

When he phoned a couple of hours later, I snapped, "It's a good thing you called."

He laughed, and said he'd change what he had booked for Wednesday. He called again on Tuesday and asked if he could see me after supper. When I got back from a dinner with a friend, Peter was sitting on my porch holding a container of ice cream. I was so happy to see him.

After he returned from Florida, we had another wonderful evening at a local Thai restaurant. A picnic in High Park, lamb sausage and couscous at Brasserie des Artistes, tapas and beer and loud Spanish music and the waitress singing and dancing in the basement of El Cid, a happy late hamburger at Fatso's. People were always smiling at us the way you do at people in love. I didn't really trust that he was in love, but I felt it.

And making love with him! He was wild, tender, controlling, docile, adventurous, spontaneous, sweet, raunchy. I loved every second in bed with him. I loved the way I could let go and fly with him. I loved the way he moved me. The way he let me move him.

During one weekend we spent in Niagara-on-the-Lake, he said, "I haven't been so happy in years. I can't remember when I last felt like this." I still didn't get it that he was in love with me. A "helpful friend" had just told me that he was in love with another woman, and that he had a reputation as a Don Juan.

To protect myself, I desperately wanted to find things wrong with him.

I trusted him absolutely as a man in my bed, but I was afraid to trust him as a man in my life. I was so in love, so in love that I could have done something crazy. But I had a strong instinct that if I married him, I would be happy for a year and miserable for the rest of my life.

It's really hard to let go of a lost love, of loss, of love. All we can do with deep feelings of sorrow is try to befriend them. Our other loves, passions, necessary duties, chosen pleasures can surround the hollow where loss lives.

Three years after I met Peter, I tore myself away from him. That summer, I participated in a shamanic weekend. My power animal "told" me, "You were not meant to be with Peter as a life partner. You came together to heal each other and yourselves. You gave each other a partner for healing. Let go of his soul. Take your own soul back. You loved Peter but you don't want him forever. Let him go. Don't keep a piece of his soul for your own energy."

Sometimes we try to clean up our past, to forget the unpleasant or difficult times, and to deny our past unhappiness or lack of compassion towards others. But if we tidy up the past, and white-wash the people and events that have profoundly shaped us, or pretty up our own actions, then we are erasing parts of our real lives, and also forfeiting the knowledge that we can attain when we survive tough times and thrive. We can remind ourselves that if we could have done something differently, we would have.

Many of us never stop loving a man we have truly loved. All those tiny filaments that bound us to him have entered our body tissue.

I have crowded my heart with memories. I have held onto pain. It's a mistake.

One way to let go of a love, after time, is by transmog-rification. If we can't rid ourselves of the feelings that cause grief and clog possibilities, we can love a past lover in a different way. We could become friends, after a while. We could "adopt" him as a brother or cousin. We could accept that he lives on in a virtual world where, in a certain way, love lives on. Or, if we're understandably pissed off at him and need to move him out of our lives quickly, we might pretend he died. (Perhaps I should mention here that I write mystery stories, so a fictional dead body is no problem. Once, after asking for his editing help, I killed my former husband in print.)

Another aid in letting go is to practice *tonglen,* the Tibetan Buddhist meditation in which we breathe in the pain of everyone suffering as we are, and breathe out wishes for their happiness. And we ask to open our hearts, in order to prepare to be able to one day love again.

What do we need to remember and what do we need to forget? Or, if not forget, hold without pain? Can we let go of attachment, let go until we are no longer bound by memories of ghosts?

A depressing and difficult passage has prefaced every new page I have turned in life. Charlotte Bronte

Journal #40: *What I need to remember.*

(Winter, 2004) The names of my people: my children, my parents and sister, nieces, friends, lovers.

Rachel's winning goals when she was the only girl in the hockey league. The times Josh made me stop the car to rescue an injured squirrel or pigeon. My mother listening to me, and feeling lifted up by her love. My father's joke, "I'm not finished, I'm Jewish—"hard to forget, heard it hundreds of times. The letter telling me that my first submitted story would be published in an anthology. The view from the Adirondack peak. The look on my ex-husband's face when we were happy. And that same look on the face of other lovers, a look of such pure trust and love. What damage have I done? I try to walk on the earth softly, but have I walked on men with cleats?

Journal #41: Your first three memories. Make each into a tiny story. Expand and rewrite in the 3rd person and forget it's you. (Alfred Adler thought that the first memories reveal the psychological leitmotif of your life.)

(Winter, 2005, Earliest Memory) Elaine was three when she fell from the porch of the Camp Naivelt cottage on the third hill. In her mind she can still see the tiny white wooden cabin and the tiny wooden porch. In that fall (the last fall she ever took without her defences in place), she cut her left palm on a piece of broken glass, just under the thumb. And that's how she learned to tell left from right.

Journal #42: A poem about a love that was well lost

Who is the keeper of the distance?
And how is it done?
The purblind push-pull
the tentacles of treacle
Blow the whistle!
Who's master of the mind-fucking
Whose voice declares
you'd better do as I want
no, you'd better do as I want
or else I'll move back
or else I'll leave
and you'll ruin it
and you'll do it wrong
again

Silver Fox Tip

Can you link lost love with lost creativity? How can you reconnect with your creative spirit?

-21-
Refuge & Travel

○ ○

The real voyage of discovery consists not of seeking new landscapes but of having new eyes. Marcel Proust

I took a teaching job in Switzerland for many reasons, the least of which was to get over a man who didn't love me enough, who wanted even more distance than I did. It took one day in Neuchatel for me to feel "over him". I was in another country, in a town constructed with local yellow sandstone that Alexandre Dumas described as "a toytown carved out of butter". My wonderful apartment, the background Alps and town lake, the *chocolateries* and *patisseries,* and making a new friend of a future colleague were a lot more compelling than a constricted relationship. A geographic change can shift you to another place, figuratively as well as literally.

Paris has been a favourite refuge. Partly because of the job in Switzerland, I have been able to go there, with not a lot of money, nine times so far. Once I spent four days alone in Paris, talking to almost no one, and wasn't lonely. I walked the streets for hours the first day, *une vrai flaneuse,* stopping to relish a glass of red wine while reading *No Great Mischief,* buying that black lace bra that made me look like a stylish pouter pigeon, sampling a *blini* at Joe Goldenberg's in the *Marais* district and then seeing William Klein's slant images of Paris demos at a nearby photography gallery. On the following morning, a café crème at the Dome on rue de Rivoli, more walking, and a free Yves Montand retrospective at the Hotel de Ville. "No wonder he was a heart throb," I thought, as I listened to old tapes of his chansons such as *á Paris* and looked at photos (poor Simone, all those pictures of her and him and Marilyn Monroe).

The next day I didn't meet Karim for breakfast. I had met him the night before at a salon on rue de Jacques, where, for 10 euros, the hosts provided tea, cakes, fruit and a meeting place for those who want to meet to talk in both French and English. The apartment was filled with attractive, mostly young people. I didn't rule myself out because of age, and the four most attractive men (all in their 30s) kept vying for my attention. At first I just thought, how nice, all these men want to practice their English. But three were fluent in English, including Karim, half French, half Persian, from Australia, an actuary, gorgeous, very funny and on my wavelength. He wore a big cross, loved soccer—he was young.

In spite of Joan Baez' song about her time in Paris with a much younger lover, the one with whom she went to the Ritz "in boots and jeans", I didn't go to the café Karim had placed on a quickly drawn map. I liked him. I knew he liked me too. That's why I didn't meet him. I was terrified of inappropriate passion. I thought how I'd love to find someone as attractive, more or less my own age, in Toronto.

Perhaps my best time in Paris was a weekend which had nothing to do with a man. I took the train from Neuchatel and my daughter flew in from Toronto, my graduation present for her. We celebrated the delicious impracticality of travelling to Paris for a long weekend with a half *caraf* of sancerre at the nearby tiny perfect Ste. Catherine Square. We didn't hit any of the tourist sites, just walked the streets, taking in the scent of coffee and fresh croissant and urine, entering small galleries to be met by artists offering more wine, and then taking tea and talk on the top floor of Shakespeare & Company. After seeing the movie, *As Good as it Gets*, we ate at the Le Grand Colbert, the restaurant where Jack Nicholson finds Diane Keaton at the romantic end of the film. I had the roast chicken the Keaton character describes as "the best in the world" (I've never had better), continuing my identification with her persona— the Annie Hall outfits, seeming flakiness, and *lah-di-dah* attitude.

I am just as happy at sanctuaries as I am in Paris. On silent meditation retreats, I feel protected by the container of a haven—protected from busyness, non-stop relating, and my frequent feeling of being stalked by time. I feel supported by many kindred spirits, all of us silent, all choosing to be together to do the practice.

Without exchanging words with any of them, I believe I know who are my friends and which people I could never like. Occasionally, I "recognize" a true soul mate and despair that I can't meet him. But he's my idealized mate *only* if I never meet him. These experiences are common on retreats, and because we don't talk to each other, it becomes clear how easily we can construct relationships and stories about ourselves and others out of little data.

There's something about the temporary nature of those interludes that reassures my fear-of-being-trapped small self. On a typical retreat I have a room of my own, get to eat gourmet organic vegetarian food, and have luxurious amounts of time and space. Even there I avoid full commitment. Ignoring the rule of keeping internal as well as external silence, I journal and read in my room. On one retreat, I even smuggled in the Sunday New York Times, bought in the nearby town and hidden in my packsack. I skip some of the sittings and go for walks, mostly mindfully, on country roads.

At Springwater Center in upstate New York, I always feel lucky to be once again in a place of beauty and peace. I've enjoyed long walks in pale yellow fields and woods of varied shades of green. Good food, conversation, hot tub. Coffee by the waterfall. Water rushes waving in thrall to a crumpled tissue paper wind. I've slept so well there.

The yurt where I took a chanting course one summer at the Jewish retreat centre, *Eilat Chayyim,* was filled with odes to joy. I was elated to be one of the voices. Ever since I was a kindergarten kid in the 1940s, when I was forced to sing a girl's alto rather than my natural bass key, my vocal insecurity and envy of those who could join campfire, car trip, or hootenannies, began.

I had been terrified to hold my song while others sang their different parts, but was helped by the early morning "Jewish meditation". The mantra which fastened us to the present was the acronym of G-d, four Hebrew letters that cannot be pronounced as a word: *yud, hay, vav, hay.* Then given further courage (as well as unexpected comedy) from "Jewish yoga", which turned out to be hatha yoga with one tiny embellishment. We ended the class in a circle of crossed legs, chanting "Sha-a-a-l–**OM**, sha-a-a-l–**OM**).

The exercise that opened my heart as well as my singing courage was the invitation to bow to "the Beloved". Although I don't believe in a traditional G-d, I bowed as a spiritual technology to get out of my head. The bow places the heart higher than the head. I could sing!

I didn't come to the retreat to open my heart; I came to mend my heart from the pain of breaking up with Anton whom I couldn't love enough. Not me, not then. I pushed him away when he got too close. He didn't feel I was in his corner, and he never called me when he was upset or needed help. We couldn't even hug each other at the end of a day without awkwardness. We both believed there was a better way to love. Now we're friends, both in new relationships.

We ended that class at *Eilat Chayyim* with a turn, a Sufi technique to spin the excess of will which might make you nauseous, or too much surrender leading to dizziness. What a great relief, not having to be in charge, not having to give way, just turning, letting yourself be turned to a still centre in the revolving world.

What constitutes a journey? If you listed all the journeys you have taken in your life, which would be inner expeditions, which outward, which both? If you drew a map of your travels, what would be on it? Who would be on it?

The map could be a blue river with jagged rocks, whirlpools, rapids and sweet spots, with chronological events and special times along the shore. It could be picturesque or picaresque, collage or single image, two or three dimensional. It could be in the form of a white road or a rainbow grid or any extended metaphor that your imagination leads you to conceive.

Have you ever gotten lost? Finding your way back when getting lost on an expedition is not only a great metaphor for the dating game, it often leads to a gain. Who hasn't been lost? Lost in love, lost in ambivalence, lost in confusion. The task of reorienting can lead to serendipitous happenings and larger horizons.

But you can't get lost, you can't get found, you can't find off-road treasures, unless you set out.

You can be your own refuge. You can learn to treat yourself as if you were the kindest parent of a beloved child. You can pamper yourself.

If you can't travel, caring for yourself when you are hurting can be as simple as slinging a camera over your shoulder and becoming a tourist in your own town, viewing the familiar with new eyes. As soon as it's possible, using a lot or little money, you can take a trip away. You can work in exchange for room and board, take a job in another country, or volunteer in a far-off place. You can travel to physical and emotional sites that provide distraction, safe haven, and possibilities for unusual engagement.

Travel can be as much fun as dating. You don't need a new man to get over a man.

The wanderer seeks many ways.
Sooner or later (s)he comes home. I Ching

The fabric of my faithful love
No power shall dim or ravel
Whilst I stay here,—but oh, my dear,
If I should ever travel! Edna St. Vincent Millay

Journal #43: *Find a significant photo from your travels. Write about the scene, remembering your emotions, food, smells, feelings...*

(Spring 2004) I'm sitting, at a wrought iron table, under a white-lace umbrella, waiting for Joe in the the hibiscus-scented courtyard of the restaurant Posada Carmana in San Miguel, Mexico. My red sandals are resting on the faded orange tiles of this former stable. Only two other women here so far, both alone, early to be dining on a Sunday at one o'clock. I feel anonymous, free, wonderful in spite of the visit of a rogue period last night, four years after I finished menopause. I'm drinking a Corona, eating a heart of palm salad with mayonnaise, and reading the latest issue of *Poets & Writers*. A folk group is playing against a background of church bells.
I met Joe the first day here at the Instituto, while signing up for Spanish classes. He is the only cute single guy in San Miguel, and he's pursuing me. I'm enjoying it, although nervous of his former life as a drug runner, his time in jail, and his family of origin. His self-absorption reminds me of mother.
I said I wanted love. Why am I so anxious about Anton coming?

Journal #44: *A true storytelling of being lost.*

The path was well signed and Elaine strode into the woods, delighting in the dappled leaves of friendly trees. After a while, she noticed that the path had narrowed and there were no markers. She attempted to retrace her steps but found no way out. She sat on a rock and breathed herself out of a panic fueled by the thought of the bears known to inhabit those north Ontario woods.

Then she thought, "I love hiking in a forest more than almost anything. I will enjoy this time. I will simply walk in one direction until I hit a road."

Elaine remained cheerful even when some brambles tore her shirt, and scraped her arm, drawing quite a lot of blood. She was able to wash off the blood in a small stream and also wash her face.

Four hours later she came upon a wide trail. She knew she was close to civilization as she stepped around clumps of horse spoor. She emerged at a clearing with two small houses.

She knocked on the bright blue door of the nearer house. A kindly looking older woman responded to her request for help with this question: "Are you single?"

Elaine nodded.

"Go next door, dear," the woman said, "and ask Gary for a ride back to your hotel. He's a lovely man—used to be a policeman in Toronto, and now he's up here teaching disabled kids."

Elaine was too tired to argue. Conscious that she was dirty, ragged, adorned with dried blood in place of makeup, she knocked on his door.

Silver Fox Tip

Think of where you wanted to go that you talked yourself out of. Make preparations to go!

-22-
What I Call Spirituality

○ ○

Let there be many windows to your soul, / ...Not the narrow pane / of one poor creed can catch the rays / That shine from countless sources. Ella Wheeler Wilcox, 1883

On her deathbed, Gertrude Stein asked, "What is the question?"

For most of my life, I only wanted The Answer.

At times, I sought purpose in the well-trodden paths of the world I was born into. I did well at school, married well, lived well, dressed well. Meaning was there, or I created meaning, for a time and space.

But in the end, I did not find the answer with a nice husband in a nice house with a nice pool.

Only once did I seek meaning in a bed, and found a very temporary answer in the arms of the lovely womanizer. The last thing I ever said to him, in a tone of furious righteousness, was, "You have no idea how monogamous people live!"

I have always been monogamous in my relating to men, and I'm still into monogamy, even hope for forever, with a human beloved. However, I have given up any wish to be true to The Big Beloved. My tenuous relationship with the guy in the sky has never inspired commitment, never survived my doubts and urge to flee.

Some women, nice women, can practice religious fidelity for a lifetime. Conversants change partners for the dance one time only. Others play around a bit before settling down. And then there are the promiscuous ones, although we prefer to be called polyamorous. It's not about always going for the romance and then cutting out; it's about searching for, not my soul mate, but my soul.

I equate finding soul with becoming as real as possible, with knowing myself better, having a sense of humour about my frailties, having more compassion and awareness. I can't help thinking all that would useful in dating. How can it be a dating disability to be real, aware, empathetic, and able to laugh at oneself? (*Memo: get hair streaked, lose 5 pounds, locate soul.*)

My mother, born into an Orthodox Jewish family in Winnipeg (her father founded a *shul* on Selkirk Street), quietly observed many traditional rituals, like lighting Sabbath candles and going to synagogue on major holidays (taking me along). When my father became a Communist in Warsaw at the age of fourteen , he renounced "the opiate of the masses". Today I lean to the left politically and am drawn to men who are either social activists or who found synagogues.

Flashback to me at five, when I loved going to Anglican Sunday School with Linda, my best friend. I especially liked colouring in the pictures of Jesus and the Disciples. When I marched for peace and cute guys in the 60s, the template kicked in. I adored disciple-looking activists.

At eight I joined the Salvation Army because I liked the way they sang. At twelve I was back into the tribal fold. I became a member of an Orthodox Jewish youth group because I wanted to belong somewhere and I liked meeting cute boys in skullcaps in paneled recreation rooms.

At sixteen I called myself an anarchist, wore a peace button and went to meetings in the basement of a Communist bookstore. More cute boys, no scullcaps.

In spite of almost non-stop seeking, I have never taken formal religion seriously enough to convert. I am Jewish, whatever that means.

At twenty-three I went to Israel, mostly because as a Jew I could work there and also take an affordable residential five-month *Ulpan* (Hebrew immersion course). When I got home from Israel, I married the son of a rabbi. That seemed to solve the two major questions of my twenties: 1) Would I ever find a husband? 2) Would I ever find a religious identity?

Soon after I left my marriage I received a sabbatical from the Toronto Board of Education to study holistic ways of teaching writing. I signed up for a writing workshop given by Natalie Goldberg at the Zen Mountain Monastery in upstate New York. On the Friday evening, before the workshop began, that boot-camp monastery taught us the basics of meditating, and then demanded an hour and a half of strict meditation. I loved it. I knew I needed it. I took to it as an anxious duck to clear water.

Meditation is a radical practice in western society because it allows us to slow down and be friendly towards ourselves—providing space for what is real. It's a process of peeling away layers of fakeness. It's about coming home to ourselves.

We respond to what is actually happening rather than what we wish were happening. We begin to understand the interconnectedness of life—in relationships, belief systems, politics. I didn't become a Buddhist (my usual lack of interest in any received dogma), but I believe in meditation.

By meditating, I saw some of my patterns immediately, noticed how my chronic worrying leads to unnecessary control. A great thing I learned from meditating is that I have enormous freedom and power to move my mind from a difficult or anxious place to a better place—to my breath, or to a Beethoven variation or a daisy petal. I can control my attention, can control its direction, wander or be still, widen it or stay narrow, be in the present, in the past or future. I also learned that control is not always negative, as had been suggested to me by some men, including a therapist. Control as well as self-control, untainted by self- absorption, can be a very good thing for a woman.

Like many mid-life women of a certain bent, I've run around to many places and sampled many practices. For many of us, having had that first marriage, raised children, done the homemaker thing, there is more space now for spiritual questing, often connected with a strong need to be in nature. In my mid-forties, I began hiking every weekend. At a workshop in core shamanism, I tried to relate to nature spirits in Algonquin Park, by talking to plants, chatting with flowers, connecting with trees.

I have my second degree in Reiki and do it almost every day. Sometimes I take classes in mellow *Iyengar* yoga or trance dancing. I dipped into Reform Judaism, complete with activist rabbi playing guitar. Stayed at a Sufi commune in Massachussets. Did work exchange for two summers at Kripalu, a Hindu sanctuary in the Berkshires. Three weekends of insight meditation in the Hockley Valley of Ontario with the Northwoods group. Meditative inquiry at Springwater Center, a kind of post-Buddhist breakaway in the hills near Rochester, N.Y. In silence for ten days at the Insight Meditation Society in Barrie, Massacheussetts. Chanted at the Jewish renewal *Eilat Chayyim* in the Catskills. Don't even ask about the holy ash I keep in a saffron-coloured cloth in my bedroom closet. Or about the Avatar who manifested the ash with his bare hands.

Perhaps all this sounds tiring and even anguished. However, because I've always accepted being Jewish without parental insistence to follow a particular religious path, I've never been tormented. I've enjoyed the searching, and have been deeply absorbed in the process.

The often moralistic advice to walk only one spiritual trail doesn't work for me. I would rather explore various terrains, taking those paths "with heart" as far as they lead me. I lack trust in the major religions, noting the secondary importance they allot to women. I want to fashion my own "religion", my own method of approaching integration and whatever enlightenment is. Another version of The Method Eclectic.

In the history of disparagement of those who cruise different spiritual roads, seekers have been criticized for lack of stability, for shallow dilettantism, for an inability to stay steadfast and true to one religious or spiritual route. But we feminist seekers can claim the right to celebrate female energy by creating our own diverse belief system.

As a woman, I want to be able to own my sexuality. As a woman spiritual seeker, I want to be able to own my own spirituality. I want to be able to both strengthen my ego and lose attachment to it, to remain a Jew, to learn from Buddhism and other religions, to do good, to escape the entrapments of patriarchy, to pay attention to myself and to the world.

We loose women are free to be ourselves. We look for the sacred in everyone and everything. Trust comes when we know we have the inner resources to withstand pressure from within and without. For me, both the sexual and spiritual paths have led to authenticity, to being genuine, to meeting whatever and whomever with fewer obstructions and more curiosity.

We realize that all relationships are an exchange of energy, but we don't feed on others like vampires, without an awareness of who they are, and we don't let others feed on us. We have choice about whom and what we want to support, and we give unstintingly. We don't play the "nice girl", "the good daughter", the "apparently pleasant girlfriend" any more. So we have more energy available for creativity in work, in life, and in love. We are able to pay attention, one of my definitions of love. Without ideological restraints, we pay attention to ourselves, to others (human and animal), nature, the person-made world, food, creative projects, the environment.

The search for a man who could trump my fears has been a little more fraught than my search for meaning through religion. So I have taken my time, and only ventured into a relationship if the man seemed good for me. I've been happy to spend years without a lover.

Perhaps I've been too careful about whom I become involved with. I have talked myself out of strong attractions, especially with men much younger than I. I wish I could have had the courage to explore my sexuality without a fear-induced chastity belt. I wanted to avoid embarrassment and pain. In doing so, it's possible I've also avoided heaven.

All the same, in the nineteen years since I left my marriage, the number of lovers has been adding up. A generation ago I would have been called a slut. Today I'm proud of my escape from societal, familial, and religious programmed sexual repression.

If we increase our ability to know ourselves and observe others through meditation and journaling, we can grow into larger spiritual beings, ready to love and be loved. We can choose what's right for us, and treat others well. We can stop looking for flaws in ourselves and each other. We can choose gratitude as our default attitude. We can embrace life without things upsetting or dominating us. We can possess paradox in this larger internal space. Hold the good and the bad at the very same time, and not call it good or bad. Sluts (of body, mind, or spirit) feel there is a lot to be said for being able to hold contradictions in the mind without needing an answer.

I've given up searching for answers. It is enough to learn how I can be the best me, the best Elaine possible for the great gift of being a life form on this earth.

Now, what is the question?

Journal #45: Gratitude exercise (inspired by Morita therapy in Japan which postulates that none of us could function as adults if we hadn't been given a lot by others and the world.) Begin with "I was given..."

(Journal, September 2007) I was given parents who would have done anything for me, but didn't know how to help me grow up. I was given a sister who was my only real intimate for a long time. A safe home. A safe country. A public school system that rescued me. I was given a healthy body, brains, and nice looks. I was given enough money. And enough love if I could have accepted it. I was given a creative drive, a gift for friendship and fun. A chance to travel. A lot of laughter.

Silver Fox Tip

Ask yourself what you would do in any given situation if you loved yourself unconditionally?

The breeze at dawn has secrets to tell you.
Don't go back to sleep.
You must ask for what you really want.
Don't go back to sleep.
People are going back and forth across the doorsill
Where two worlds touch.
The door is round and open.
Don't go back to sleep. Rumi

-23-
Letting Go

○ ○

We must be willing to let go of the life we have planned, so as to have the life that is waiting for us. E.M. Forster

Freedom comes from not hanging on/ you've got to let go, let go
Freedom comes from not hanging on/ you've got to let go, let go
Freedom, we will have our freedom
Freedom, we will have our freedom

> (Chant taught to me by Sophia, a west coast
> witch, when I was teaching a journaling
> course in Northern British Columbia.)

Letting go of controlling others is a challenge for some of us. Difficult to finally get it that not only can I not control his behaviour, I can't even control my wanting to control his behaviour.

Why do I teach the practice of letting go? Probably because at least a hundred times a day, when I'm pushing someone to see my point of view or to take my advice, I could say, *STOP—LET IT GO.* I worry about worrying, regret too much, keep trying to have things go my way, keep doing too much. But I'm less controlling than I used to be, back when I thought I was a flexible somewhat easy-going person.

When I'm in a state of anxiety about an aspect of a man's behavior that should only concern him, I still sometimes cross that line and tell him how to be. To get back to balance, I think of a person I know who always tells you what to do, and then I think of someone who is more easygoing. I imagine myself as each woman, and experience what it is like to be even more bossy than I am, and then to be able the kind of person who lets others live their own lives.

We think we can be safe if we can just get everything in order, everything in place, and keep it that way. However, since change is inevitable, the best we can do is to just live one moment at a time. We don't have to fix everything, solve everything. We can just hang out, not grasping safety, not anticipating the next moment, the next bite of food, the next ego hit.

One of the lovely ah-ha moments of my life was when I really got it that I was never going to be "together". I think that almost all of us can be both wonderful and terrible. When I understood this I realized I didn't have to work any longer at perfection. I can learn from just living, from talking to friends, working, and reading and writing a little. I can relax and be my own fabulous fucked-up sweet self. I can stop pretending to be cooler than I am. And I can let go of expectations of another's perfection.

Others often resist our transforming into a genuinely more easy-going person. They may have resented our interference, but they can feel abandoned when we give them space to make their own decisions. They may wonder if we are moving on. Sometimes all they need from us is reassurance that we are not planning to leave them behind as we grow. Often our living demonstration of change will cause change in them too. Certainly it works better than nagging or proselytizing. (I learned that the hard way—two boyfriends have called me "A Major Nag").

Yet sometimes we must leave someone behind. We might find that we can't relate any more to a lover or friend who is playing in the sandbox when we're graduating from college. We can't love out of guilt or historical affection.

I also have been learning how to be less apprehensive before and after I'm involved with a man. I can put my attention wherever I want: in my breath, onto a tree, into a Coltrane tenor sax piece, with my dance steps. I give myself time. I need time to know if a man is good for me.

Instead of expressing my anxiety by bickering or picking at him, I can ask him for reassurance, ask for information, or check an assumption.

To relax into more acceptance of *what is,* we can affirm the possibility of change. The crucial shift comes when the desire to change is greater than the fear of the process. When we become aware of how tightly wound we are, we must be patient. We might resist a new idea that threatens us. If we let the energy of this new concept flow by itself, we become accustomed to its pace. We find ourselves relaxing into each moment.

We can release, sometimes in tiny amounts, anger, resentment, bitterness, and self-demeaning habits, as well as beoming more conscious of our self-destructive behavior—in my case, habits such as eating a great deal of pastry, sipping a little too much wine, indulging in that extra cup of strong coffee, voracious reading, gossiping, and neurotic explaining.

Letting go is being able to clear the enmeshment of old loves with compassion. Perhaps we can change the form of the relationship. Played-out sexual tension can allow former lovers to be great friends.

Transitions can be hell. Our beloved dies or leaves or we leave and are alone. But each new hell burns off more illusions. If we can let ourselves surrender to the pain, to the poignancy of loss that accrues as we age, we can recreate our ways of relating to ourselves and the world. It's true that some of us never stop loving the men we love, but we eventually wear out our capacity to suffer over them.

Through journaling, you can become more aware of what and whom you have to let go of. You can transcribe intentions to drop burdens and habits. You can vow to throw out bits and pieces of psychic weight from your heavy packsack until you can walk through the world with a lighter step.

By journaling, you are giving birth to yourself. Your words form a birth canal. The labour and delivery might be tough, but a great dame is being born.

You can't prevent sorrow from flying over your head, but you can prevent him from building nests in your hair.

Chinese Proverb

Journal #46: Write an ode to letting go.

(November, 1996)
Bound to the bedposts by compulsion
I turn my head and stare
at my two shelves of books whose main message is
LET GO
I have meditated
breathed in bravery breathed out what I didn't need
written LET GO a hundred times in my journals
I don't want to be a tortured kind of person
I admire those who commit
and clear clutter courageously
I can do it with clothes, books, semi-beloved objects
so why do I still mourn all my loves?
Today I phoned my doctor to ask if she would take my ex-husband
as a patient
dined with my last lover last week
and my present one yesterday
the one who delights me with his need for space

Here's the new rule: Break the wineglass, and fall toward the glassblower's breath. Rumi

Journal #47: 21 Day Exercise

This exercise in non-attachment to one's thoughts or self-image was given during the month I spent at the Zen Mountain Monastery in upstate New York. We were instructed to go to the same place every day and sit for an hour. I went to the pond. Day after day I sat on the same comfortable chair-shaped rock. I learned that going to the same place at the same time for the same period of time can help us see the fluidity of life. I realized that my thoughts kept changing and the world also kept changing. Everything is always changing. The belief in the "truth" of our thoughts or the naïve hope that the world can stay the same just causes us suffering.
(August 2000, The Zen Mountain Monastery)

Day 1   A blood red dragonfly landed on one of the rocks beneath my home rock. The water lilies are gone. Just some petals amongst the leaves. There is almost no wind today. I can feel a breeze on my face, but the pond is almost still except for the ping of bugs in their playground. I find myself asking, "Why am I with Michael?"

Day 6   The pond is brown today and the reflections of the trees leaning to the water are troubled. Even the museum white clouds look muddy in the moving water. A frail wind bends and bows the long grasses. A spider, this spider with a ruby belly, dances across home rock. Yesterday the white lily, as folded and bright as love, vanished. Today there is another flower like an origami fan, among its spinach green raft of leaves, their undersides a surprising sienna. And the bugs still play, sometimes together.

Day 14   What happens doesn't matter as much as how I meet my life. The pond is a dirtier brown today. The yearning trees are troubled. Michael will always be out of reach.

Day 15   Haiku
the pond is brown today
reflections of trees are troubled
white clouds are muddy in the dull mirror

Silver Fox Tip

Meditation encourages us to decide how we wish to direct the mind for a period of time. I invite you to breathe, imagining each inhalation as a caress, an invitation to open and soften, each exhalation as a discharge of toxins. We know something about the fruits of meditation: stress management, deepening levels of self-acceptance, ability to tolerate what used to be intolerable, calmness, clarity, a mind that is not obstructed. It isn't easy to arrive at these states, and impossible to stay in them always, but even if we have many more seconds of what I might call enlightenment, it's worth the effort.

After a great pain a formal feeling comes—
This is the Hour of Lead —
Remembered, if outlived,
As freezing persons, recollect the Snow—
First Chill—then Stupor—then the letting go.

Emily Dickinson

-24-
True Love

○ ○

In real love you want the other person's good. In romantic love you want the other person.

Margaret Anderson (editor of
The Little Review in the 1920s)

I have talked to men and women who had given up hope of ever finding true love—and only then found it. How can we explain this phenomenon? In some cases a refusal to settle for less than what we desire rewards us with a soul mate, one we could have missed out on without the space and availability created by the tough choice to refuse half a love. Relinquishing our ego's demands for validation through *ersatz* love brings us peace and the inner calmness to choose well. Perhaps giving up the need to have our lives be "saved" by a lover brings a corresponding acceptance and cherishing of our actual lives, a pleasure in living that results, among other things, in our being highly attractive. Whatever the reasons, there is hope for all of us who wonder if we'll ever find what we're looking for.

Meeting a true love might be as much about when as whom. Sometimes we overlook a wonderful person because we are not able to see what he has to offer. When we aren't ready for the genuine stuff, we can become infatuated with someone who glitters but is not gold. We bring an attitude to each encounter with a new man. We usually meet and love someone on the same emotional level as we are. If our own level changes as we live and grow and grow up, if we are lucky, if we are ready, if the stars are aligned, if he is someone who could be good for us, there is a special moment when we start a lovely love story.

Whatever real love is, it is not always easy. It is not nice. It is a process, often frightening, of learning how to grow in the presence of the other, how to help the other grow into his best person as well. This process is sometimes subtle and gentle, sometimes brutal and fierce.

A couple can truly commit to their relationship if each is prepared to suspend some cherished attitudes. Even, at times, put off or put on hold what they think of as their absolute needs. When we give up our ego's wishes, fantasies and illusions, we can honour the great unknown of the relationship. We can share the mystery and become a strong team.

What does it mean to be loved? I feel loved when I feel safe, defended, supported, special, belonging, cared about, and accepted. I must keep in mind that my companion probably has similar longings.

We expect that our relationship should make us feel good. Often it does, and then "ain't life grand." Sometimes it can't, and when it can't, we blame the other, and love turns to not-love. During those times, it is better to experience and accept the pain and disappointment, to lean into it, to let yourself really get it that nothing is perfect and that your partner does not have the job of always pleasing you.

A relationship becomes important not because it satisfies personality needs but when it's a pathway to wholeness. Only when we allow for our own pain can we be sympathetic to the other's pain, even when he's acting it out in unpleasing ways.

If both persons involved learn how to tell their truths to each other, and if they can be vulnerable with one another, they can be of extraordinary reparative service to each other.

Each will feel known, each helped to release self delusion, each less lonely. They can become real in the container of the relationship, can act imperfectly and laugh and forgive. They can love and feel loved. They can have an adult relationship instead of perpetually longing for an unconditional love that, in my opinion, exists nowhere. (Okay, maybe when I was nursing my babies, we each felt that kind of boundless love. Maybe in a bed it happens for a fleeting wondrous while, maybe it happens for no reason at all for a few seconds, or hours, or even months. But never for always. Never all of the time.)

While we are learning how to love a man, we rarely move up a linear ladder. Often as we complete a cycle of learning, the next rung reveals another, perhaps better, set of problems.

The pain of emotional separation becomes worse the closer we get to each other. At some point we might find it's worth it to look at our own contribution to any disconnection rather than blaming the other. The bad feelings can then shift and melt, and we might begin to feel empathy for both of us. We might even be able to laugh and compost crappy arguments into private jokes. There's no better comedic material than our own contributions to relationship craziness, and no better love glue than busting up over them (instead of breaking up because of them).

Don't, as I have in the past, run away as soon as you're uncomfortable. If you stay, sometimes bearing acute discomfort, that can be a choice to love. When I've had an argument with the man I love today, instead of staying separate and self-righteous I try to hang in there with the feeling of misery until the right action presents itself. I am choosing not to unbolt an escape hatch, not to have the usual one foot out the door. (This counsel holds as long as you are with a good person. If you have sound reasons to suspect the person you are with is abusive, then you need to do what you can to make yourself safe. Staying with an abusive man is another way that we cheat ourselves from experiencing real love.)

It's an illusion that a woman can "make a relationship good", as my mother recommended. We can only relate, and try not to present as nicer than we actually are. We're cheating the other if we portray a sweeter, less angry version of our selves. If we give who we are, we can experience the joy of true connection. We can help the other through our genuine responses. We can sometimes be a mirror for his imperfect behavior (as he can ours), thus opening a channel to growth.

When we have rigid expectations of another person we create an arena for failure ("if he really loved me, he would…"). Most inflexible expectations are detrimental to a relationship. However, for many of us, sexual fidelity must be honoured for trust to grow. It is useful to ask yourself if your expectations limit intimacy or encourage it.

I am learning to keep my mouth shut about my partner's issues, particularly the ones I'm certain are true. (Does anyone really want to hear unsolicited psychological advice from a lover?) I'm allowing myself to be vulnerable and ask for reassurance instead of attacking—the only skills I had before were angry confrontation or flight. I'm learning to accept his reality, even when his reality is very different from mine. When I feel like demanding something of him, I'm trying to express a preference instead of a claim. Trying to love through a problem rather than battle through it. All this sounds good, but it's hard work. The triumph is that I can occasionally manage to do it.

And sometimes, even in the middle of a rage, I can remember my partner's good qualities and cool down. When I'm at my best, what I define as semi-enlightened, I am able to let my lover's mistakes fall away, let them all go in thirty seconds. The reward is my feeling good instead of bad and mad at myself, and my lover can relax a bit more with me. He need not "walk on eggshells."

Whenever a man declared commitment, my pattern used to be to stall and then freak out. I'm not passive-aggressive in most situations, but that one was a giant challenge. In response to his declaration of wanting forever with me, I would say something like, "Oh, well, let's see what happens". Within the next twenty-four hours, I would inevitably regress to one of my childhood tantrums, scream for help to a god I don't believe in, and scare the guy away, at least an emotional distance away. I didn't seem to be able to say, "I just can't commit, not to anyone right now." When I cried after pushing a man from me, I always felt ashamed, abandoned, unloved, alone.

To counter my reactive nature, I use a technique suggested by Nora, the Celtic shaman. I lean back into my spine, do Kegel exercises (it's hard to spit out something nasty while my vagina is working out). I have learned to ask, "What do you mean by that?" instead of pouncing. His answer often tells me that my touchy assumption was wrong.

I still don't know how to love as well as I would like. It's hard for me to relate to someone without trying to change him. I have attempted to educate lovers about some of the following irritations: chewing gum, investing money wildly, keeping his place too neat, or too messy, having different politics from mine, playing golf—and being too controlling!

I want to be able to share thoughts and feelings with the people I love, not need to change them. Here are some questions for me to remember to ask. "Do I understand you enough? In what way could I be there more for you?"

Instead of looking for love, I recommend searching yourself for things within that hinder intimacy and choosing to engage in the struggle to reduce them. From time to time you can check if you are causing unhappiness or frustration for another. You can simply ask your partner "Is everything okay?"

But of course we can look for love as well. For the first nine years of my singledom, I waited for love to find me. But just before and right after I came back from teaching in Europe, I decided to throw out a large net, with the idea of meeting and releasing as many fish as I needed to before keeping the catch I wanted. I put an ad in the personal section of the Saturday Globe & Mail, and registered on three internet dating sites, and asked friends to fix me up. Mocking myself, I nonetheless lit a red candle in the south west corner of my apartment (the love corner, according to a *feng shui* book*)*.

There are so many possible models of mating today in North America. We can be openly polyamorous, and have several lovers, serious or casual, but all warm and caring. We can be monogamous within a traditional marriage, or within an *amitie romantique,* in which we merge little, live apart, see our children separately, even take some vacations by ourselves, but maintain our commitment to be a couple. We can marry but not live together, live together and not marry, live in neighbouring houses or apartments, share a house with separate apartments or have separate bedrooms (with visiting rights). We can live in the same city or town or have a continuing long distance relationship. I considered marrying my first post-marriage romantic love on the condition that I could have a yellow room—with a lock. In our winter years, women and men can have more freedom to design their way of being together.

Real love teaches you how to love as you go along because there are no pat solutions. You're always bumping against your edge because you know you are not going to leave. You have chosen not to escape.

When romance ends, when disappointment dawns, true love might have the chance to begin. We don't know where the relationship is going but we're strapped in for the ride.

When the heart is flooded with love there is no room in it for fear, for doubt, for hesitation. And it is this lack of fear that makes for the dance. Anne Morrow Lindberg

__Journal #48:__ If there is a man you want to be closer to, ask yourself: What troubles or difficulties have I caused him? How can I be more sensitive to his needs? How has he gone out of his way to please me?

Silver Fox Tip

Magic for drawing love to you: Start texting your beloved-to-be in your journal. Believe he is out there and ready to meet you. Feel the connection. Visualize the happy relationship.

Until one is committed, there is hesitancy, the chance to draw back, always ineffectiveness, concerning all acts of initiative (and creation). The moment one definitely commits oneself, then Providence moves, too.

   A whole stream of events issues from the decision. Whatever you can do or dream you can, Begin it. Boldness has genius, power and magic in it. Begin it now.

W.H. Murray, The Scottish Himalayan
Expedition (usually attributed to Goethe)

-25-

the write time, the right man, the right you

○ ○

Live in each season as it passes; breathe the air; drink the drink; taste the fruit; and resign yourself to the influence of each...Open all your pores and bathe in all the tides of nature, in all her streams and oceans, at all seasons.

Henry David Thoreau

And now our journaling circle is coming to an end. I thank you for writing with me. Where do we go from here? What are the possibilities?

As we read over our journals, we can go to another level of learning about ourselves. We become aware of what stories we have been telling ourselves. We can observe how we created those stories. We can see that they are not necessarily true, although we believed them at the time. We can perceive how we were asleep, or unconscious. Now we are more awake. A year from now we might even be more awake.

We can witness, in writing, our pessimism, our optimism, our egotistic moments and our times of shame.

We can ask, "What is the voice in my journals like?" Am I strident, or irritable, or too placid? Am I witty? Weak, ineffectually repetitive, or silly? Strong or falsely tough? Intimate with myself, or protected and distant, even formal?

171

We can read our continuing themes. My themes are obvious—they are the chapters of this book. What are yours? Regret? Ambition? Joy? Distrust of love? Rage against men?

What are the images and symbols that reoccur? In my journals, there are a lot of roads, some rivers, the play of light and dark, all the old chestnuts. You might want to track your images to discover more information about yourself.

What are your reoccurring thoughts? Are you surprised by anything when you read over one of your journals? I was taken aback to find that, in spite of all those Buddhist retreats, I was incredibly judgmental of my lovers. Perhaps you will see more generosity than you give yourself credit for, or more anger than you have ever acknowledged. I found more sadness than I knew I had—my self-image is of a mostly happy person.

What is uncomfortable to read? Our own bad behavior, or the way we let ourselves be stepped on? Our rationalizing, or our critical natures? Whatever it is that makes us cringe has energy, and that's worth exploring.

So how can we get to another layer of truth? On rereading our journals, we can tune into what we are presently feeling as we look over past emotions. We can write responses to what we are reading. We can see where we have come from. We can figure out where we are now and where we appear to be going.

We can be more proactive in designing our lives. We can change course. We can imagine ways of emerging into who we want to be. We can write new scripts to get there.

If we have the intention to live a more truthful life, we will grow to be the women we were meant to be. That is, more and more real. There may be times when we can't speak our truths entirely—if we are working for an impossible boss, planning to escape a violent partner, or talking to a parent with dementia. But ultimately our intention needs to include being as honest and authentic as possible, with ourselves and others. The more we can do that, the stronger our self-esteem, the better we can date successfully.

What do we have to let go of so that something else can be born in our lives? There's no time left to waste on what weighs us down, what sucks our energy, or who isn't in our corner. No time to waste, so best to believe in ourselves and to live well.

Journaling can help awaken us from trance states. I was in somewhat of a trance when I got married, when I was raising my children (at least until I started understanding how I was asleep at the mommy wheel), and while dating in the first years after my marriage ended. I was under a spell during the times I was fretting (without taking action) about the world's problems. I still sometimes act like an automaton, gorging on sweet things or gossip, indulging in worry and small irritations.

I was able to break some of these trance states by a variety of means: speaking from a vulnerable place to someone trusted, writing without editing, meditating, allowing myself to feel pain too uncomfortable to feel before, and by realizing that I was causing someone to suffer. And learning to give myself time before making a decision or before over-reacting.

Think of your work, both in journaling and relating to men, as freeing yourself from limiting beliefs, and beginning to let go of chronic dramas, of fixed and limited fabrications, in order to find the more genuine story. You are getting ready to be squarely inside your life. You are preparing to meet whatever comes to you, whether heartbreak or astounding happiness.

What do you consider to be a happy ending? Is it a deep marriage, or a live-in or live-out partner? Do you yearn for a sometime lover who is also a friend? Would you prefer a companion in another country? Does your happy ending include several casual fun lovers who leave you with lots of free time? Or does your good life have no lover at all? How do children, friends, work, projects, and passions fit into your dreams?

You have the means to find out. All you need is you, attitude, and pen and paper.

Journal #49: *Read one of your journals as if you were a detective of your own life. What clues are there? Is there evidence of unskillful patterns? What surprised you?*

Journal #50: *Write "A Letter to the Universe", giving thanks (in advance) for bringing you the love you want.*

(Summer, 2006) Thank you for manifesting my perfect partner in my life now. He is kind, loving, tender, sincere, generous, faithful, refined, intelligent, has a similar diet and attitude to health, a great sense of humour, he's expressive, he likes to travel, he's thoughtful and gets who I am. He's available, fun-loving, healthy, sensuous, sexy, supportive of me and my work, enjoys the arts. He's ready for a commitment and has similar interests. He's functional, emotionally healthy, has worked through his stuff, has a spiritual side, cares about people, is easy to be with, has dreams, likes his work (or avocation), and respects my boundaries.

A true conception of the relation between the sexes will not admit of conqueror and conquered; it knows but one great thing; to give of oneself boundlessly, in order to find one's self richer, deeper, better. Emma Goldman

Silver Fox Tip

The 12 step program for finding love

1) Keep a dating diary.
2) Go for more personal power.
3) Choose gratitude as a default position.
4) Become ready to receive love.
5) Remove your blocks to the kind of love you wish for.
6) Find out what you really want in a lover.
7) Always tell the truth, but do it gently.
8) Pay attention to yourself, others, and the world.
9) Imagine having it all, whatever all is.
10) Let go of what you don't need any more.
11) Don't expect perfection.
12) Have patience.
13) Write a letter to the Universe, asking for a lovely lover.

If you obey all the rules, you miss all the fun.

Katherine Hepburn